Ronald Blythe, *writer*

I called upon God, and the spirit of wisdom came to me ... For she is the brightness of the everlasting light, the unspotted mirror of the power of God, and the image of his goodness. For she is more beautiful than the sun, and above all the order of stars: being compared with the light, she is found before it.

The Wisdom of Solomon, 7: 7, 26, 29, Apocrypha (AV)

Favourite Wisdom

CHOSEN BY PEOPLE FROM
ALL WALKS OF LIFE

Compiled by
Deborah Cassidi

WITH WOOD ENGRAVINGS BY
A.J. CUNDALL

continuum
LONDON • NEW YORK

Continuum

The Tower Building

11 York Road, London SE1 7NX

15 East 26th Street, New York, NY 10010

www.continuumbooks.com

First published 2003

British Library Cataloguing-in-Publication Data
A catalogue record for this book is available from the British Library.

Library of Congress Cataloging-in-Publication Data
Favourite wisdom: chosen by people from all walks of life/compiled by Deborah Cassidi;
with illustrations by Jackie Cundall.
    p.cm.
Includes indexes.
ISBN 0-8264-6085-2 (pbk.)
    1. Conduct of life–Quotations, maxims, etc. 2. Wisdom–Quotations, maxims, etc. I.
Title: Favourite wisdom. II. Cassidi, Deborah.

BJ1581.2.F34 2003
170'.44–dc21   2003055250

ISBN 0-8264-6085-2

Designed by Geoff Green
Typeset by Geoff Green Book Design
Printed and bound by MPG Books Ltd, Bodmin, Cornwall

To my father Rupert Bliss whose presence is in *Favourite Prayers* and who lived in God's grace.

My thanks to the many contributors, to my long-suffering friends and family and to Judy and Barbara; also to Jane, Maggie, Frank, Phillipa and Chris in the Somerset Libraries' Arts and Information Service, and in particular to my husband. This book would not have been possible without their help.

Contents

⸏⸏⸏⸏⸏⸏⸏

List of Abbreviations

ASB	Alternative Service Book (1980)
AV	Authorized Version of the Bible (the King James Bible)
NRSV	New Revised Standard Version of the Bible
1928 Prayer Book	The Prayer Book as proposed in 1928
RSV	Revised Standard Version of the Bible

It is a pleasure to commend such an interesting book with contributions from a variety of people of all ages. Their choices of *Favourite Wisdom* reflect a wide range of experience and extend from thoughts of a thousand years ago to the present day. The result is a stimulating collection which I hope will provide much inspiration and enjoyment.

Lady Elizabeth Gass, Lord Lieutenant of Somerset

Foreword

~~~~~~~~~~

Anyone who knows *Favourite Prayers* (Continuum, 1998) compiled by Deborah Cassidi will be eagerly anticipating this new collection of *Favourite Wisdom*. In an age swamped by myriad electronic communication, wisdom can seem to have a rather archaic image, even if on the quiet we are all looking for it. The contributors from many walks of life have chosen a broad kaleidoscope of wise sayings, poetry and humour. Sometimes you turn the page and there is one of your own favourites which has supported you through anxiety, grief or decision, and then on the next page there is a totally new thought which is good to explore.

Many of the selections have a fascinating context, which further illuminates the saying. Sir Michael Palliser quotes Dietrich Bonhoeffer who was hanged in Flossenberg concentration camp on 9 April 1945. Sir Michael adds, 'I spent that day in my tank advancing along the north German plain shortly before the German capitulation – it was my 23rd birthday.' Sometimes it is wisdom passed on by a parent, teacher or friend and treasured from childhood. Sometimes it is drawn from that essential ingredient of the good life – positive humour. I like Michael Brearley's choice, 'Don't just *do* something, stand there!' Maeve Binchy's anonymous poem rings an alarm-bell with me, and it was a treat to see Lord Runcie's comment, 'The Church is like a swimming pool; the splashing goes on at the shallow end.' (Not just the Church?) I also enjoyed learning from the choices of other celebrities – such as Gary Lineker's 'Circumstances do not determine a man, they reveal him.' There are treasures of faith from many sources. The overall experience is an affirmation of goodness, an incentive to battle on against adversity and a recognition of faith, hope and love as the foundations of true wisdom.

I have begun to realize that compiling an anthology is no easy task. This one offers us the gift of a window into other people's proven philosophies. As Jesus showed by affirming the choice of the two great commandments from a bewildering multitude of regulations, laws and moral imperative, right selection is the key to wisdom!

THE RT REVD JAMES THOMPSON

The Making of the Anthology

Compiling this book has been a joy and a privilege and I thank the contributors with all my heart. They have sent me treasured quotations from chests and diaries, from kitchen walls and family letters; wisdom received in childhood, gleaned in passing or hammered on an anvil of adversity; wise advice from parents, teachers and friends.

The quotations are arranged chiefly in alphabetical order of contributor. When a quotation was chosen by more than one person, I allocated it to the first nominator, adding other names as they came in. It was decided at the onset only to use titles and honours coming before the name. This had the advantage of simplicity, but it saddened me that some awards for bravery and honours of distinction were left out. I apologise for this, and to those who sent pieces which I could not include either because I could not obtain copyright, or because the viewpoint had already been covered, or because the piece was beyond the scope of this book.

Comments by the contributors appear in quotation marks; my own editorial remarks are preceded by the symbol ¶. The author or source, when known, follows each contribution, and publication details are given in the Acknowledgements on p. 166. Sadly, due to the variability of sources and the constraints of space and copyright, it was not always possible to include the full text or particular wording supplied by the contributor.

I guessed from the outset that this book might be more challenging than *Favourite Prayers*. For a start, there was the problem of the definition of 'Wisdom'. Collins Dictionary mentions 'the ability to use knowledge, erudition or enlightenment; a wise saying or teaching; also soundness of mind'. The Standard Oxford English

Dictionary adds 'the capacity of judging rightly', and 'one of the manifestations of the divine nature in Christ'.

Rather daunted, I gave the contributors the option of something spiritual or secular, serious or funny, long or short, reflective or practical. As their letters arrived, I saw the depths of my ignorance and how much more there was to the subject than the dictionary definition. Colin Davis said of a Meredith poem, 'For me it is "wisdom" as is the seventh symphony of Sibelius, although I cannot prove it.' I found again and again that the boundaries were nebulous; that wisdom blends into prayer, truth, beauty and the mysterious. The themes of love, responsibility, endeavour, hard slog, generosity, honesty, friendship, death and our relationship with God and each other were recurrent. But difficult subjects such as greed, recalcitrance, sin, prejudice and war were also tackled. Perhaps I learned that wisdom is there to help us on our journey to our awesome end with less fear. So if the reader finds that the corner of a curtain has been lifted to give a glimpse of the unexpected, the humorous or the mysterious, then the task will have been justified.

There are certainly omissions from the book. If a mathematical reader would propose a piece of numerical wisdom I should add it to another volume. My father might have suggested the asymptote, that strange line which I am told will meet its parallel in infinity. I have no vote for the golden mean, the mathematical foundation of so much beauty.

The youngest contributor is Flora, who gives some guidelines for health services on who should be allowed to bounce on the beds. The oldest is Walter Leach, aged 104, who advises us to appreciate the works of others. I should have included a rebellious teenager to put their turbulent point of view. There is much about marriage, but I must include an extract from Samuel Pepys' diary, dated 6 January 1663.

> Only, myself somewhat vexed at my wife's neglect in leaving her scarf, waistcoat and night-dressings in the coach today that brought us from Westminster, though I confess she did give them to me to look after – yet it was her fault not to see that I took them out of the coach.

The stuff of marriage, but how he loved her.

Collecting permissions and copyright has been the usual juggle.

I can only gasp at the generosity of writers and copyright holders who gave without stint and with their blessing. I thank them so very much. Finding, at the last moment, an email from the 92-year-old Czeslaw Milosz giving permission with his blessing for 'And Yet the Books' was a special joy, as was the opening of the letter from the Dalai Lama with his contribution. There was no such happy outcome to my attempt to contact Aung San Suu Kyi. She had emailed Alan Clements the text of a poem by Rabindranath Tagore, saying that it gave her great comfort. I was unable to verify the translator of her version and by the time I found a translation by Tagore himself it was not possible to contact her. She remains under house arrest, a veritable prisoner, and the poem remains a testament to her courage. On the triumphant side again is the message from Archbishop Tutu, 'God loves us ' … It is enough.

The Duchess of Abercorn

〜

We have one infallible guide, and only one: the Universal Spirit which inspires each and all of us, implanting in every individual a yearning for what ought to be – the same Spirit which causes the tree to aspire towards the sun, which causes the flower to shed its seeds in autumn and which impels us instinctively to draw closer together.

Leo Tolstoy (1828–1910), from 'Lucerne', a short story published in 1857

Roger Ableson, *builder, born Saltburn, Yorkshire*

〜

'If in doubt, say nowt.'

Sir Antony Acland, *former Provost of Eton College*

〜

All that is necessary for the triumph of evil is that good men do nothing.

Sir Edmund Burke (1729–97)

¶ Attributed, in various forms, to Burke, although not found in any of his works.

Charanjit AjitSingh, *lecturer and writer*

Awake in peace
Stay in peace
There is no fear
With such understanding.
One God is our master, our saviour
Who knows the hearts and minds of all.
Sleep carefree, awake carefree
Because here and beyond, you abide O Lord!
Peace prevails at home
Peace abounds outside
Nanak says, 'Because the Guru has taught the practice.'

Guru Granth Sahib, from *The Wisdom of Sikhism*, trans. Charanjit AjitSingh
(standard page 1136)

❡ The *Guru Granth Sahib,* or *Adi Granth,* is the first volume of the Sikh scriptures. It is treated with great devotion and is divided into standard pages of equal length. The contents are mainly intended for singing.

HRH Princess Alia Al Hussein of Jordan

'There are various bits of advice which have been a help over the years, but I think they come down to doing your best and leaving the rest in God's hands. The main thing is to have genuinely good intentions behind our actions and not wallow in despair when things seem to go against our wishes. They often turn out to have been in the best interests of all. I believe there really is a "greater plan" of the Almighty, and have been privileged to feel proof of this on many occasions. A seemingly tiny detail sets in motion – or prevents – a series of other larger and smaller events and one sits back in awe at the intricacy of the "providential pattern".

The Qu'ran shows that you may hate what is good for you and wish for what is evil for you, but God knows and you know not! We are sometimes obsessed with a plan and battle away to no avail. God lets us try our hardest, and waits until we acknowledge our inability to force the issue. He answers when called upon to help us. In Islam, God is also named "The Hearer, He who Responds to prayer".

A final word – an idea expressed by the Imam Al Ghazali in his work *Ihya' ulum al deen* [The Revival of Religious Sciences] – we often do things which we know are wrong, or of no value, to impress others. The time will come when what others thought of us is of no value and the opinion of the very One who saw everything now counts.'

¶ Imam Al Ghazali (1058–1111), Sufi philosopher and poet.

Peter Alliss, *golfer and broadcaster*

Give me a good digestion, Lord;
And something to digest.
Give me a healthy body, Lord;
And sense to keep it at its best.
Give me a healthy mind, O Lord,
To keep the good and pure in sight
which seeing sin is not appalled,
but finds a way to put it right.
Give me a mind that is not bored,
that does not whimper, whine or sigh.
Don't let me worry overmuch
about this funny thing called I.
Give me a sense of humour, Lord,
the grace to see a joke;
to get some happiness from life
and pass it on to other folk.

Thomas Henry Webb (1898–1917)

¶ Webb based this poem on words discovered in Chester Cathedral. He died on the Somme on December 1 1917.

Elizabeth Allsop, *retired smallholder*

It's what you do that makes you what you are – not what you talk about doing.

'A Bostonian American whom I knew in Edinburgh gave me this. I lost touch with her years ago when she returned to the USA, but she braced me up when I was rather down.'

Never ride slack – see any hazards before your horse does.

W. R. Brown, banker (d. 1947)

'This was from my late father. You don't need a horse to find this useful!'

Lord Armstrong of Ilminster, *retired public servant*

Advice given by the old cat to the young kitten:
'Always purr when you're pleased.'

'My "favourite wisdom", learnt from my father many years ago.'

The Very Revd Dr John Arnold, *Dean Emeritus of Durham Cathedral*

If the beast who sleeps in man could be held down by threats – any kind of threat, whether of jail or of retribution after death – then the highest emblem of humanity would be the lion-tamer in the circus with his whip, not the self-sacrificing preacher. But don't you see, this is just the point – what has for centuries raised man above the beast is not the cudgel but an outward music: the irresistible power of unarmed truth, the attraction of its example. It has always been assumed that the most important things in the gospels are the ethical teaching and commandments. But for me the most important thing is the fact that Christ speaks in parables taken from everyday reality. The idea which underlies this is that communion between mortals is immortal, and that the whole of life is symbolic because the whole of it has meaning.

Boris Pasternak (1890–1960), from *Dr Zhivago*

Carol Auger, *market-stall holder*

Who would true valour see,
Let him come hither;
One here will constant be,
Come wind, come weather.
There's no discouragement
Shall make him once relent
His first avowed intent
To be a pilgrim.

Who so beset him round
With dismal stories,
Do but themselves confound;
His strength the more is.
No lion can him fright,
He'll with a giant fight,
But he will have the right
To be a pilgrim.

Hobgoblin nor foul fiend
Can daunt his spirit:
He knows he at the end
Shall life inherit.
Then fancies fly away,
He'll fear not what men say,
He'll labour night and day
To be a pilgrim.

John Bunyan (1628–88), from *The Pilgrim's Progress*

Professor M. A. Zaki Badawi,
Principal of the Muslim College, UK

⌒

And, lo, Luqmān spoke thus unto his son, admonishing him: 'O my dear son! Do not ascribe divine powers to aught beside God: for, behold, such [a false] ascribing of divinity is indeed an awesome wrong!

And [God says] We have enjoined upon man goodness towards his parents:

[Revere thy parents;] yet should they endeavour to make thee ascribe divinity, side by side with Me, to something which thy mind cannot accept [as divine], obey them not; but [even then] bear them company in this world's life with kindness, and follow the path of those who turn towards Me. In the end, unto Me you all must return; and thereupon I shall make you [truly] understand all that you were doing [in life].'

'O my dear son,' [continued Luqmān] 'verily, though there be aught of but the weight of a mustard-seed, and though it be [hidden] in a rock, or in the skies, or in the earth, God will bring it to light: for, behold, God is unfathomable [in His wisdom], all-aware.

O my dear son! Be constant in prayer, and enjoin the doing of what is right and forbid the doing of what is wrong, and bear in patience whatever [ill] may befall thee: this, behold, is something to set one's heart upon!

And turn not thy cheek away from people in [false] pride, and walk not haughtily on earth: for, behold, God does not love anyone who, out of self-conceit, acts in a boastful manner.

Hence, be modest in thy bearing, and lower thy voice: for, behold, the ugliest of all voices is the [loud] voice of asses …'

Advice of the Sage Luqmān to his son, from *The Message of the Qur'an*. 31st Surah, vv. 13–19, trans. Muhammed Asad

George Baker, *actor*

⌐

Are you in earnest? Seize this very minute.
What you can do, or dream you can, begin it.
Boldness has genius, power and magic in it,
Only engage!

John Anster (1793–1867), Professor of Civil Law at Trinity College, Dublin.
Derived from Goethe's *Faust*.

Also chosen by **Lady Marion Fraser.**

Joan Bakewell, *broadcaster*

POLONIUS: ... Give thy thoughts no tongue,
Nor any unproportion'd thought his act.
Be thou familiar, but by no means vulgar.
The friends thou hast, and their adoption tried,
Grapple them to thy soul with hoops of steel;
But do not dull thy palm with entertainment
Of each new-hatch'd, unfledg'd comrade. Beware
Of entrance to a quarrel: but, being in,
Bear't that the opposer may beware of thee.
Give every man thine ear, but few thy voice:
Take each man's censure, but reserve thy judgment.
Costly thy habit as thy purse can buy,
But not express'd in fancy: rich, not gaudy:
For the apparel oft proclaims the man ...
Neither a borrower, nor a lender be:
For loan oft loses both itself and friend,
And borrowing dulls the edge of husbandry.
This above all: to thine own self be true;
And it must follow, as the night the day,
Thou canst not then be false to any man.

William Shakespeare (1564–1616), from *Hamlet*, Act I, Scene iii

'Polonius is often portrayed as a doddering old fool, but this is the sort of sound advice any parent might give to a child about to become a student.'

Also chosen by:

Dennis Silk, *retired headmaster and former President of MCC and the TCCB, who said, 'Shakespeare had a habit of putting sound advice in the mouths of otherwise idiotic or pedantic people. My elder brother made me learn this off by heart before I went back for my last year at Christ's Hospital to be Head of School.'*

Thelma Holt, *actress, wrote that two quotations (lines 4–5 and 18–20) were 'deeply embedded in my heart'.*

Sir Ludovic Kennedy, *writer and broadcaster, who chose the last three lines of this speech.*

The Rt Revd Peter Ball and the Rt Revd Michael Ball

The last thing to leave the heart of a servant of God is the love of power.

Muslim saying

The Church is like a swimming pool; the splashing goes on at the shallow end.

Most Revd Robert Runcie (1921–2000)

Helen Bamber, *founder and Director of the Medical Foundation for the Care of Victims of Torture*

It seems to me that true religion begins with the law about protecting and shielding the alien and the stranger. It's there in practically every religious tradition and it is there that men and women discover the idea of humanity.

Voltaire said that if we believe in absurdities, we shall commit atrocities. And if we believe in the absurdity that people who are fleeing their country, their home, their families, their job are doing it for a whim, we will be on the way to committing the atrocities.

How you are with the one to whom you owe nothing; that is a grave test and not only as an index of our tragic past. I always think that the real offenders at the half way mark of the century were the bystanders; all those people who let things happen because it didn't affect them directly.

I believe that the line our society takes on how we are to people to whom we owe nothing is the critical signal that we give to our young. I hope and pray that is a test we shall not fail.

Rabbi Hugo Gryn, CBE (1930–96), from 'A Moral and Spiritual Index'

'I reflect on the words of Hugo Gryn because he used his own experience of atrocity and massive loss (he lost his entire family and everything they possessed) to understand and reach out to present victims of repression, whoever and wherever they are.'

¶ The Medical Foundation works with survivors of torture and organized violence, both adults and children. It provides medical therapies and advice, and trains health professionals and others to work with survivors of torture. It also campaigns against torture and works to improve the legal framework for treatment of asylum-seekers and refugees.

Priscilla Barker, *housewife*

Good water; good life. Poor water; poor life. No water; no life.

Peter Blake (1948–2001)

¶ Peter Blake, for whom this was a guiding belief, led 'Team New Zealand' in two successive America's Cup victories. He aimed to increase awareness of issues vital to the planet's survival and was killed defending his crew on the River Amazon in December 2001.

Shamba Barnett, *capoeira dancer and school mentor*

⤿

Move faster, work harder … at least there is no blood like in Brazil.

Mestre Pastel, Groupo de Capoeira, Raizes de Rua, London

I once asked a friend why he thought Capoeira was so unusual and difficult to learn. Without a pause for thought, he said: 'In the West we stand up and we sit down. Occasionally if we drop something we bend over. Sometimes we run and every night we lie flat on our backs. Outside there are few movements that we perform frequently, so, in Capoeira, where all the movements are circular and we spend so much time off the ground, it doesn't surprise me that people who aren't brought up with it find it difficult.'

Florence Royer, Groupo de Capoeira, Raizes de Rua, London

❡ Capoeira is a Brazilian martial art dance which may have originated 400 years ago in Angola. The Brazilian slaves and the impoverished urban inheritors of their tradition disguised their forbidden movements of aggression and self-defence as an elaborate dance. Every step must be controlled and dignified. A combatant shows an offence, then moves gracefully out of the way, showing submission. He then takes the upper hand, using a vast range of interlocking, fluid and acrobatic kicks or stances. It is a game of tact, guile, cunning and reflex.

Sebastian Barry, *playwright*

Aa, a mhac: ná bí ag briseadh báid.

[Ah, son: don't be breaking boats.*]

'The saying has a force whose nature is elusive. The boat was beautiful in its time. It dealt with the house-high waves of the Atlantic. Leave it in memory of its usefulness. Memory remains a blueprint of things that might one day need urgent remembering.'

¶ Perhaps this enigmatic quotation has links with tradition in the West of Ireland. A friend of mine was reminded of the following quotation from *The Only True History of Lizzie Finn* by Sebastian Barry:

'Every district has its custom by which a district endures. You must revere the custom of the place or die away. You must turn the warm sheaves to the sun obediently, or die away.'

The character, Bartholomew, is referring to a lost custom in his part of County Kerry where the mistress of the house 'would come out from the house to the hay lying dry as dresses in the field, and take up the pitchfork like a very man and turn the first line to the sun for luck. For luck in the harvest and in the going on of things.'

*The saying features in the poem 'Gaeltacht' by Pearse Hutchinson:

> A Dublin tourist on a red-quartered strand
> Hunting firewood found the ruins of a boat,
> Started breaking the struts out – an old man came,
> he shook his head, and said:
> 'Aa, a mhac: ná bí ag briseadh báid.'
> [Ah, son: don't be breaking boats.]

Professor John Bayley, *author and retired Professor of English Literature*

~

 T ake short views – never further than dinner or tea.

Revd Sydney Smith (1771–1845)

'This advice given by the Revd Sydney Smith to a disheartened and greatly worried parishioner is often, and justly, quoted. It is advice that does work, or so I found when looking after my wife, Iris Murdoch, who was terminally ill with Alzheimer's disease.

It was no use lying awake wondering what to do, or what would happen next. Instead we embraced and laughed together – she would always respond in kind to laughter and smiles. She loved to be told a joke, as I suppose a child might do, even if she did not understand what it was about. Speech and smiles were the great thing.'

*Also chosen by **Sir Patrick Nairne**.*

The Rt Hon. Tony Benn, *politician*

The Furies

War is the mistress of enormity,
Mother of mischief, monster of deformity;
Laws, manners, arts she breaks, she mars, she chases,
Blood, tears, bowers, towers, she spills, smites, burns and razes.
Her brazen teeth shake all the earth asunder:
Her mouth a firebrand, and her voice a thunder,
Her looks are lightning, every glance a flash,
Her fingers guns that all to powder smash;
Fear and despair, flight and disorder, post
With hasty march before her murderous host.
As burning, waste, rape, wrong, impiety,
Rage, ruin, discord, horror, cruelty,s
Sack, sacrilege, impunity and pride
Are still stern consorts by her barbarous side;
And poverty, sorrow and desolation
Follow her armies' bloody transmigration.

Joshua Sylvester (1563–1618), London merchant, translator and writer

Mary Bennett, *former Principal of St Hilda's College, Oxford*

⌒

After leaving Burdwan at the Commencement of my Journey in my Travelling carriage I found the road very bad – there had been a heavy fall of rain – & it was like so much deep sand or Mud. I often thought I should have to remain all night. The Coachman was a Mild tempered man, & did not use the Whip, & the Syce who accompanied the Horse first patted the Animal, then spoke to him in the most coaxing manner calling him his Brother, Sister, etc., told the Horse he had not far to go, to try this once to excel himself, and by dint of help at the wheels and coaxing the Horse we at last got through our difficulty and reached the end of our six-mile stage. The next stage was equally hard, & the syce not so ready with his tongue but a harsh man & he beat the poor Animal & so we stuck fast and must have remained if we had not got the help of some people by the road to raise the Carriage out of the swamp and help us on. Every day brought fresh instances of the different Kinds of management made use of in getting the Horses along and I invariably remarked that it was the same as in Human life, & that Persuasion, firmness and Kindness always did most in effecting its end. Tho to be sure there were one or two instances where a good whipping was a very effective stimulus.

From a letter from Dr John Jackson in India to his daughter in England 1854. Quoted in Mary Bennett, *Who was Dr Jackson? Two Calcutta Families: 1830–1855*

Mary Berry, *cookery writer*

⌒

The best thing a man can do for his children is to love their mother.

Sir Michael Bett, *businessman*

~

Speak to the earth and it shall teach thee.

Job 12: 8. (AV)

'Nearly 60 years ago an elderly canon from Salisbury Cathedral preached a sermon at my prep school. I don't remember exactly what he said, but the text stuck in my mind. Today it is my heraldic motto. For me, those words are a reminder that, as good and beautiful things spring from the earth, I would be wise to seek out what the earth has to teach me.'

¶ Sir Michael also gives an interpretation that leaders should have the modesty to seek to learn from the wisdom and experience of those at the grassroots of an enterprise.

Brian Bevan, *retired coxswain of Spurn Point Lifeboat, Hull*

~

Friday flit; short sit.

'This is an old seafarer's saying which I have often used. It warns us never to start any major *new* venture on a Friday. For instance, I would not start to move house on a Friday and on the three occasions when I travelled south to collect a new lifeboat I was careful not to set out on a Friday – we do not count this as affecting a call-out as we are already in service.'

¶ Brian Bevan has one gold, two silver and two bronze lifeboat medals for bravery. On St Valentine's Day 1979 he and his crew rescued four men from a Panamanian coaster. The wind was blowing severe gale to storm force, with driving snow. The operation took 35 minutes. They turned to leave and within two minutes the coaster rolled over and sank.

The Royal National Lifeboat Institute Charity is on 24-hour standby and in one year alone rescued 6,400 people from the sea.

Maeve Binchy, *writer*

So far today,
I've done all right.
I haven't gossiped,
lost my temper,
been greedy
or grumpy,
been nasty,
selfish or overindulgent.
I'm very thankful for that …

But in a few minutes, God,
I'm going to get out of bed.
And from then on,
I'm probably
Going to need a lot more help.

Anon.

The Rt Hon. Lord Bingham of Cornhill, *Senior Law Lord*

Johnson … You know, humanly speaking, there is a certain degree of temptation which will overcome any virtue. Now, in so far as you approach temptation to a man, you do him an injury; and, if he is overcome, you share his guilt.

James Boswell (1740–95), from *The Life of Samuel Johnson*

The Rt Hon. Tony Blair, *prime minister*

∽

Seize the day
(*Carpe diem*)

Horace (65–8 BC), *Odes* I, xi, 8

❡ 'Even while we speak, Time, the churl, will have been running. Snatch the sleeve of today and trust as little as you may to tomorrow.' (I, xi, 7–8)

Also chosen by **Admiral Sir Michael Layard.**

Colonel John Blashford-Snell, *explorer and scientist*

∽

Be cool in crisis and decisive in action.

Arthur Wellesley, 1st Duke of Wellington (1769–1852)

'The selection process for an expedition is very important. To find out if someone possesses courage I try to discover if they have fear, for one who does not have fear can have no courage: they do not need it. Such folk do exist and can be frightening company, often leading their comrades to take unnecessary risks.

Next, I see if the candidate has willpower, because in many cases I believe courage is resolute willpower. As well as physical courage, there is moral courage, the sort that will lead one to stake all on your own judgement. Strangely, those who appear to possess unbounded bravery do not always display moral courage. On the other hand, I have never known a person who has moral courage to be found wanting in the face of physical danger.'

Lady Blelloch, *retired teacher and civil servant's wife*

Give me the ability to see good things in unexpected places, and talents in unexpected people. And give me, O Lord, the grace to tell them so.

From 'Growing Old Gracefully', also known as
'Seventeenth-Century Nun's Prayer'. Anon.

Rabbi Lionel Blue, *liturgical scholar, writer and broadcaster*

When I am examined at the gate of the world to come they won't enquire as to why I was not Moses but as to why I was not Zusya …

Rabbi Zusya, Hasidic master

¶ The Hasidic revivalist movement started in Poland in the eighteenth century following the Chmielnik massacres. It taught that God was to be found everywhere and could be served in everyday activities.

Each community was led by a charismatic leader, such as Rabbi Henoch. They were believed to work miracles and to be channels for divine energy.

Julian Bond, *Chairman of the National Association for the Advancement of Coloured People*

༐

Just do something you can live with.

Revd Ralph Abernathy (1926–90)

'It was 1966 and I was faced with a dilemma. I had been elected to the lower house of the Georgia General Assembly with a few other African-Americans, the first of our race to be so elected. Our presence was controversial, to say the least.

Shortly before our swearing-in, I endorsed a statement critical of American involvement in the Vietnam War. A storm of protest and a movement to exclude me arose. I was faced with a dilemma: retract the statement – which I strongly believed in – or insist upon it and face certain expulsion.

A day before the final decision had to be made, I ran into the Revd Ralph Abernathy, Martin Luther King's closest friend. He gave me this advice: "Just do something you can live with."

I stuck by my statement, and was expelled. After a long battle I finally took my seat and served in the legislature for the next 20 years.'

Lord Melvyn Bragg, *writer and broadcaster*

Blessed are the poor in spirit, for
   theirs is the kingdom of heaven.
Blessed are those who mourn, for
   they shall be comforted.
Blessed are the meek, for they shall
   inherit the earth.
Blessed are those who hunger and
   thirst after righteousness, for they shall be
   filled.
Blessed are the merciful, for they
   shall obtain mercy.
Blessed are the pure in heart, for
   they shall see God.
Blessed are the peacemakers, for
   they shall be called the children of God.
Blessed are those who are persecuted
   for righteousness' sake, for theirs
   is the kingdom of heaven.
Blessed are you when men shall revile
   you and persecute you, and shall say all manner
   of evil against you falsely for my sake.
Rejoice, and be exeedingly glad: for great is your reward
   in heaven, for so persecuted they the
   prophets which were before you.

Matthew 5: 3–12 (AV)

Revd Marcus Braybrooke, *President of the World Congress of Faiths*

I will give you a Talisman.
Whenever you are in doubt,
or when the self becomes too much with you,
apply the following test:
  Recall the face of the poorest
and weakest man whom you may have seen
and ask yourself if the step you contemplate
is going to be any use to him.
  Then you will find your doubts
and your self melting away.

Mahatma Gandhi (1869–1948)

On my way to the Mosque, O Lord, I passed the Magian in front of his flame, deep in thought, and a little further I heard a rabbi reciting his holy book in the synagogue, and then I came upon the church where the hymns sung gently in my ears and finally I came into the mosque and pondered how many are the different ways to You – the one God.

Ibn (al-)Arabī (1165–1240)

¶ Ibn (al-) Arabī was a Sufi mystic who studied in Seville. He taught that all existence is a manifestation of the divine substance. Considered a heretic, he was marked for assassination. He also said, 'Love is the faith I hold and whereso'er his camels turn, the one true faith is there.'

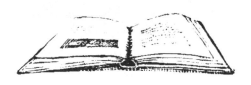

Michael Brearley, *psychoanalyst and retired cricketer*

ᔈ

Don't just *do* something, stand there!

'This advice was given by his senior doctor to a junior doctor in a psychiatric ward, when he was frantically trying to respond to people and pressures from all sides.

I enjoy the humour, and find it invaluable as advice in many contexts of life. We are so often pulled into activity, whether to retaliate, or make amends, or to be seduced to side with someone. And these days there is even more of a sense of urgency. What is lost, however, is the capacity to take in what is going on, to reflect, to be there for the complainer, the seducer or the person in need.

The junior doctor was Tom Main, a psychoanalyst who became Director of the Cassell Hospital, Surrey. Neither he nor I would advocate passivity, but it is often hard to be still and really take in the other's state of mind.'

Willie Bremner, *retired cooper*

ᔈ

It's nae aye the tightest hoop
That makes the cask hud in.

'In order to keep the wood impermeable to the maturing whisky, the curved staves of a barrel are cut from the width not the length of an oak tree. The skill of the cooper lies in judging the curve of the staves and fitting them together with exact precision. No amount of tightening of the hoops will overcome shoddy workmanship.'

Sean Brophy, *management consultant and writer*

⌒

I thank God for the wonder of you, and you and you.

'An old friend of my mother was guest of honour at a dinner which re-united them after 60 years. He proposed this unusual toast as grace.'

The Rt Hon. Lord Browne-Wilkinson,
Senior Lord of Appeal in Ordinary

⌒

On the opening of the then new Law Courts by Queen Victoria, the judges prepared a loyal address which started (some may think pompously): 'Conscious as we are of our manifold short-comings …' A very distinguished judge objected to this opening, saying that he was not conscious of any shortcomings, let alone manifold ones. At this another equally distinguished judge suggested that the difficulty could be overcome by substituting for the offensive phrase: 'Conscious as we are of each other's manifold shortcomings …'

Darcey Bussell, *ballet dancer*

⌒

'Always laugh at your mistakes.'

Professor Sir Kenneth Calman, *Vice-Chancellor and Warden of the University of Durham and retired Chief Medical Officer*

❧

Never trust a doctor whose house-plants die.

William Carden, *diplomat*

❧

If I was young and handsome as I was, instead of old and faded as I am, and you could lay the empire of the world at my feet, you should never share the heart and hand that once belonged to John, Duke of Marlborough.

> Sarah, Duchess of Marlborough's reply to the Duke of Somerset's proposal some years after the death of her husband to whom she had been happily married for 45 years.

'Courage, constancy, kindness. Three of God's gifts to mankind. Constancy is becoming less common. So mankind becomes poorer. Advice for my children – and myself? Remember the Samaritan. Go out of your way to be kind.'

Sir Richard Carew Pole, *President of the Royal Horticultural Society*

❧

The kiss of the sun for pardon,
The song of the birds for mirth,
One is nearer God's heart in a garden
Than anywhere else on earth.

Dorothy Frances Gurney (1858–1932), from 'The Lord Planted a Garden'

The Rt Revd and Rt Hon. Lord Carey of Clifton,
former Archbishop of Canterbury

⌒

Ask, and it will be given you; seek, and you will find; knock, and it will be opened to you. For every one who asks receives, and he who seeks finds, and to him who knocks it will be opened. Or what man of you, if his son asks him for a loaf, will give him a stone? Or if he asks for a fish, will give him a serpent? If you then, who are evil, know how to give good gifts to your children, how much more will your Father who is in heaven give good things to those who ask him? So whatever you wish that men would do to you, do so to them; for this is the law and the prophets.

Matthew 7: 7–12 (RSV)

Rear Admiral James Carine, *Past Master of the Worshipful Company of Chartered Secretaries, member of the Copyright Tribunal and horse-racing steward*

⌒

It is better to remain silent and be thought a fool, than to speak out and remove all doubt.

Abraham Lincoln (1809–65)

The critical period in matrimony is breakfast time.

A. P. Herbert (1890–1971), from *Uncommon Law*

The Hon. Dame Silvia Cartwright, *Governor-General of New Zealand*

So many gods, so many creeds,
So many paths that wind and wind,
When just the art of being kind
Is all this sad world needs.

Ella Wheeler Wilcox (1850–1919)

Deborah Cassidi, *retired doctor*

O wad some Power the giftie gie us
To see oursels as others see us!
It wad frae mony a blunder free us,
And foolish notion.

Robert Burns (1759–96), from 'To a Louse'

'Given to me by my father when I was a child and not properly attended to.'

Jesus did not come to explain suffering but in order to fill it with his presence.

Paul Claudel (1868–1955), French poet and dramatist. Quoted by Donald Nichol in
The Testing of Hearts, a Pilgrim's Journal

Admiral Sir Desmond Cassidi, *retired naval officer*

It is upon the navy under the Providence of God that the safety, honour, and welfare of this realm do chiefly attend.

Charles II (1630–85), from the preamble to the Articles of War

'This quotation is inscribed above the entrance to the Royal Naval College, Dartmouth.'

Professor Owen Chadwick, *historian*

Love is swift, pure, religious, happy and pleasant. It is strong, and patient, and faithful, prudent and long-suffering. It has the strength of humanity. It never goes after what is to its own advantage.

If one of us is out for good to the self, it is failure in love. Love thinks before it decides. It is upright, yet with humility. It is not weak, nor a frivolity, nor a hunter after the trivialities of the world. It is chaste and stable.

Love is quiet. It does not let the senses run away with it. It is thankful to God and trusts and hopes even when it seems not to find God. Without suffering no one can live as a loving person.

Thomas à Kempis (1380–1471), from *De Imitatione Christi* [*Of the Imitation of Christ*] Book 3 Chapter 5. Published *c.* 1424

The Rt Revd and Rt Hon. Richard Chartres,
Bishop of London

T o the untrained eye, ego climbing and selfless climbing may appear identical. Both kinds of climbers place one foot in front of the other. Both breathe in and out at the same rate. Both stop when tired. Both go forward when rested. But what a difference! The ego climber is like an instrument that's out of adjustment. He puts his foot down an instant too soon or too late. He is likely to miss a beautiful passage of sunlight through the trees. He goes on when the sloppiness of his step shows he's tired. He rests at odd times. He looks up the trail trying to see what's ahead even when he knows what's ahead because he just looked a second before. He goes too fast or too slow for the conditions, and when he talks his talk is forever about somewhere else, something else. He is here, but he is not here. He rejects the here, is unhappy with it, wants to be farther up the trail, but when he gets there will be just as unhappy because then 'it' will be 'here'.

Robert Pirsig (1928–), from Zen and the Art of Motor Cycle Maintenance

Beth Chatto, *gardener and writer*

M ay you, just once or twice in your lifetime,
see something infinitely rare and strange
and beautiful.

I wish you delight of plants – the small miracles
of graft and cutting, seed and bulb and corm. Of
new life from the earth.

I wish you the gloom of the garden in winter
– and, after months of anticipation,
the small, green signs of Spring.

Pamela Brown (1928–), from 'Nature's Gifts'

Hewitt Clark, *retired lifeboat coxswain, Lerwick, Shetland Isles*

Life is about making decisions, often difficult ones. As Coxswain, I dreaded being faced with an impossible rescue. I told myself I would never turn back unless the risk of losing my crew were greater than that of saving those in need. Thankfully, I never had to make that decision.

❡ Hewitt Clark holds a gold, silver and three bronze lifeboat medals for gallantry. He has worked in Force 11 gales and in 1995 rescued 60 Russians who leapt from a rope-ladder strung between their stricken ship and the Trebister Ness rocks. His brother, son and nephew are also lifeboat men.

The Lerwick lifeboat was launched 20 times in the year 2000 alone.

Alan Clements, *author*

⤻

You young people who came to this university to acquire educational skills that will enable you to build respectable lives for yourselves, I hope you will take away with you the capacity to build for others as well as yourselves …

We live, we make mistakes, we suffer and we learn. That is the cycle of life we have to follow. Where will you go from here, with your pristine young lives ahead of you? I have no words of wisdom to offer, no words of infallible advice that will enable you to avoid the pitfalls of human existence. I would wish you a happy journey, one that is free from trouble and defeat. But such fortune is not ensured to all of us. So for those of you who will have to face the usual – and at times more than usual – quota of disappointment and sorrow, I would like you to remember on the darkest nights of your storm that there are those who do not know you, but who understand your trouble and who care, because they themselves have known the absence of a comforting light. And in those times when your lives are full of light, I would like you to think of the ones who are deprived of the basic requirements of a meaningful existence, those who dare to hope that salvation is around the corner.

From a letter sent to South African students by Aung San Suu Kyi, Burmese
pro-democracy leader and Nobel Peace Laureate

Alone

If there is none who comes when you call, walk alone.
If there is none who speaks, and they turn aside their
pale faces, bare your heart and speak alone.
If there is none to share your journey,
and they all leave you and go,
tread upon the thorns of your path and bleed alone.
If there is none to light the lamp in the stormy night,
and they shut their doors against you,
light your own heart with thunderflame, and burn alone.

Rabindranath Tagore (1861–1941)

¶ Aung San Suu Kyi wrote that she took strength from this poem by Tagore. Because of her imprisonment it has not been possible to gain her permission to use these quotations.

Alan Clements is the author of *The Voice of Hope*, a book of conversations with Aung San Suu Kyi.

Dr Stephanie Cook, *pentathlon Olympic champion, Sydney 2000*

⌒

They that wait upon the Lord shall renew their strength; they shall mount up with wings as eagles; they shall run and not be weary; they shall walk and not faint.

Isaiah 40: 31 (AV)

'This verse has always been a great source of strength and encouragement to me, and often helped me to give of my best in the final running phase of modern pentathlon competitions.'

Andrew Cooney, *youngest person to reach the South Pole*

⌒

'Achievement is not what people expect or think of you, it's about having a dream or a goal and achieving it despite setbacks and adversity.'

¶ The South Pole lies 730 miles from the Antarctic coast. Andrew, aged 23, reached it in January 2003.

Sir Henry Cooper, *heavyweight boxing champion, European and British titles, 1959–70*

⤚

The only thing we have to fear is fear itself.

Franklin D. Roosevelt (1882–1945), 1st inaugural address, March 1933

Jilly Cooper, *writer*

⤚

Trust in the unexpected.

Mark Twain (1835–1910), from *The Adventures of Huckleberry Finn*

'This was the watchword of Huckleberry Finn as he embarked on his journey down the great Mississippi River. I think it's a wonderful motto, because it means have faith in the future and don't worry. Your life will often get better, and things will suddenly happen to cheer you up. You go out on a grey morning and suddenly in a bleak hedgerow you see a patch of snow-drops and it truly lifts the heart.'

Be comforted little dog. Thou too in the Resurrection shall have a tail of gold.

Martin Luther (1483–1546)

'I find this very beautiful, because it assumes that animals have souls and that one will meet them again in an afterlife.'

Helen Cresswell, *writer*

It is a dangerous error to confound truth with matter-of-fact. Our life is governed not only by facts, but by hopes; the kind of truthfulness which sees nothing but facts is a prison for the human spirit. To kill fancy in childhood is to make a slave to what exists, a creature tethered to earth and therefore unable to create heaven.

Attributed to Bertrand Russell (1872–1970)

At the four corners of a child's bed stand Perseus and Roland, Sigurd and St George. If you withdraw a guard of heroes you are not making him rational; you are only leaving him to fight the devils alone.

G. K. Chesterton (1874–1936)

Anne Crossley, *compliance reviewer*

⁓

On Marriage

Then Almitra spoke again and said, And what of Marriage, master?
And he answered saying:
You were born together, and together you shall be forevermore.
You shall be together when the white wings of death scatter your
　　days.
Ay, you shall be together even in the silent memory of God.
But let there be spaces in your togetherness,
And let the winds of the heavens dance between you.

Love one another, but make not a bond of love:
Let it rather be a moving sea between the shores of your souls.
Fill each other's cup but drink not from one cup.
Give one another of your bread but eat not from the same loaf.
Sing and dance together and be joyous, but let each one of you be
　　alone,
Even as the strings of a lute are alone though they quiver with the
　　same music.

Give your hearts, but not into each other's keeping,
For only the hand of Life can contain your hearts,
And stand together yet not too near together:
For the pillars of the temple stand apart,
And the oak tree and the cypress grow not in each other's shadow.

Kahlil Gibran (1883–1931), from *The Prophet*

His Holiness the Dalai Lama

For as long as space endures
And for as long as living beings remain,
Until then may I too abide
To dispel the misery of the world.

From the Buddhist text of *Bodhisattvacharyavatara*
[A Guide to the Bodhisattva's way of Life] by the Indian scholar-saint, Shantideva

Brian W. Daniels, *organ-builder*

All these rely upon their hands and each is skilled in his own work. They keep stable the fabric of the world and their prayer is the practice of their trade.

Ecclesiasticus 38: 31, 34, Apocrypha (RSV)

'Organ-making, like other similar crafts, is a fertile ground for errors for the slack mind; there is a need for constant vigil on past, present and possible future activities, whatever you're doing.'

Sue Darling, *housewife*

Sin is behovely,* but all shall be well and all shall be well and all manner of thing shall be well. And thou shalt see for thyself that all manner of thing shall be well.

Julian of Norwich (*c.* 1342–post 1416)
Revelations of Divine Love, Chapter 27

❡ Other sayings of Julian's include, 'God is our Mother as well as our Father'; and, of Christ, 'Love was his meaning.'

*Inherent in humanity.

Gavyn Davies, *Chairman of governors of the BBC*

Sport is a wonderfully democratic thing, one of the few honourable battlefields left. Its values should be treasured and protected.

Danny Blanchflower (1926–93)

Sir Colin Davis, *conductor*

〜

Simply the thing I am shall make me live.

William Shakespeare (1564–1616), *All's Well That Ends Well*, Act IV, from Scene iii

Love's Grave

Mark where the pressing wind shoots javelin-like,
Its skeleton shadow on the broad-backed wave!
Here is a fitting spot to dig Love's grave;
Here where the ponderous breakers plunge and strike,
And dart their hissing tongues high up the sand –
In hearing of the ocean, and in sight
Of those ribbed wind-streaks running into white.
If I the death of Love had deeply planned,
I never could have made it half so sure,
As by the unblessed kisses which upbraid
The full-waked senses; or failing that, degrade!
'Tis morning; but no morning can restore
What we have forfeited. I see no sin;
The wrong is mixed. In tragic life, God wot,
No villain need be! Passions spin the plot;
We are betrayed by what is false within.

George Meredith (1828–1909), Sonnet no. 43, from *Modern Love*

'For me the poetry is grand and full of wisdom which cannot be expressed in any other way. Analyse it as we may, Meredith has a prophetic gravity that no one can miss. For me it is "wisdom" as is the seventh symphony of Sibelius, although I cannot prove it.'

Serena de la Hey, *artist and sculptor in willow*

If I have seen further it is by standing on the shoulders of giants.

Sir Isaac Newton, in a letter to Robert Hooke, 5 February 1675/6

¶ Serena de la Hey's huge Willow Man is a familiar sight to anyone passing Bridgwater when travelling in the West Country.

Christopher Dean, *schoolboy*

If there be righteousness
in the heart, there will be
beauty in the character.
If there is beauty in the
character, there will be
harmony in the home. If
there is harmony in the
home, there will be order
in the nation. When there
is order in each nation,
there will be peace in the
world.

Reputed to be an old Chinese saying

Sophie Decaudaveine, *soprano*

⟿

SONYA: What are we to do? We must go on living! We, Uncle Vanya, must go on living. We shall live out a long succession of days and endless evenings. We shall suffer with patience the trials fate sends us; we shall work for others, now and in our old age, and know no rest. And when our time comes we shall die, humbly; and beyond the grave we shall tell how we suffered and wept, and how bitter our life was, and God will take pity on us. And then, Uncle dear, you and I will come to see a bright and beautiful, exquisite life. We shall rejoice, and we shall look back on our present unhappiness with a tender smile and we shall find rest. I believe it, Uncle, I believe it ardently, passionately … we shall find our rest.

We shall rest! We shall see the heavens aglitter with diamonds; we shall see all earthly evil, all our sufferings drowned in a grace which will flood the whole world. And our life will come to be as gentle, soft and tender as a caress. I believe it, I do … Poor, poor Uncle Vanya, you are crying … [through her own tears]. You have known no joy in your life, but wait, Uncle Vanya, just wait … we shall rest … we shall rest!

We shall rest!

Curtain

Anton Chekhov (1860–1904), from *Uncle Vanya*, end of Act IV

Paul Dee, *Professor of Radiology*

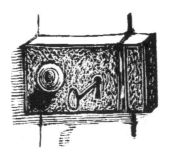

Of all things, banish the egotism out of your conversation, and never think of entertaining people with your own personal concerns or private affairs; though they are interesting to you, they are tedious to everybody else: besides that, one cannot keep one's own private affairs too secret. Whatever you think your own excellencies may be, do not affectedly display them in company; nor labour, as many people do, to give that turn to the conversation, which may supply you with an opportunity of exhibiting them. If they are real, they will infallibly be discovered, without your pointing them out yourself, and with much more advantage. Never maintain an argument with heat and clamour, though you think or know yourself to be in the right; but give your opinions modestly and coolly, which is the only way to convince; and if that does not do, try to change the conversation, by saying, with good humour, 'We shall hardly convince one another; nor is it necessary that we should, so let us talk of something else.'

Dr Samuel Johnson (1709–84), in a letter to Philip Dormer Stanhope,
4th Earl of Chesterfield

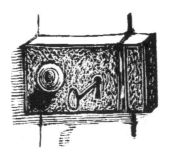

Caroline Dennis, *housewife*

I thank Thee, God, that I have lived
In this great world and know its many joys;
The song of birds, the strong, sweet scent of hay
And cooling breezes in the secret dusk,
The flaming sunsets at the close of day,
Hills, and the lonely, heather-covered moors,
Music at night, and moonlight on the sea,
The love of kin and fellowship of friends,
And all that makes life dear and beautiful.
I thank Thee, too, that there has come to me
A little sorrow, and sometimes, defeat,
A little heartache and the loneliness
That comes with parting, and the word 'Goodbye'.
Dawn breaking after dreary hours of pain,
When I discovered that night's gloom must yield
And morning light break through to me again,
Because I know that there is yet to come
An even richer and more glorious life.
And most of all, because Thine only Son
Once sacrificed life's loveliness for me –
I thank Thee, God, that I have lived.

Elizabeth Craven

❡ No information could be found about Elizabeth Craven.

General Sir Jack Deverell

⤳

Question not, but live and labour
Till your goal be won,
Helping every feeble neighbour,
Seeking help from none;
Life is mostly froth and bubble,
Two things stand like stone
Kindness in another's trouble
Courage in your own.

Adam Lindsay Gordon (1833–70), from 'Ye Wearie Wayfarer. Hys Ballad, in Eight
Fyttes', Fytte 8. Also to be found on Gordon's headstone

'A master at my school would often use the last four lines of this poem. I found it by accident 40 years later, and was reminded of him and the sentiment that the verse encapsulates.'

Also chosen by **William Carden.**

Leadership is a mixture of example, persuasion and compulsion, but in fact it is mainly you.

Viscount Slim (1891–1970)

'Most definitions of leadership are rather complex. To me, this is the shortest, clearest and most complete.'

¶ William Joseph Slim was the second son of a Bristol iron-merchant. According to Lord Mountbatten, 'Slim was the finest general the Second World War produced.' It was Slim's brilliance that turned the tide against the Japanese in Burma in 1944. Despite his apparent ruthlessness he was kind and approachable, with a quiet sense of humour, inspiring immense confidence and possessing tremendous fortitude.

Nadir Dinshaw, *writer*

～

The Empress Helena (mother of the Emperor Constantine) at Bethlehem for the feast of the Epiphany muses on the visit of the Magi to the Infant Jesus

Helena was dead to everything except the swaddled child long ago and those three royal sages who had come from so far to adore him.

'This is my day,' she thought, 'and these are my kind.'

'Like me,' she said to them, 'you were late in coming. The shepherds were here long before; even the cattle. How laboriously you came, how odd you looked on the road, attended by what outlandish liveries, laden with such preposterous gifts!

'Yet you came, and were not turned away. You too found room before the manger. Your gifts were not needed, but they were accepted and put carefully by, for they were brought with love.

'You are my especial patrons,' said Helena, 'and patrons of all late-comers, of all who have a tedious journey to make to the truth, of all who stand in danger by reason of their talents.

'Dear cousins, pray for me,' said Helena, 'and for my poor overloaded son. May he, too, before the end find kneeling-space in the straw.

'For his sake who did not reject your curious gifts, pray always for the learned, the oblique, the delicate. Let them not be quite forgotten at the Throne of God when the simple come into their kingdom.'

Evelyn Waugh (1903–66), from *Helena*

'I have chosen this extract from Evelyn Waugh's *Helena* for two reasons – firstly because I myself am, by birth, a Zoroastrian, so the Magi are my spiritual ancestors, and secondly because I find it very moving that Waugh, who might be thought to be steeped in class-consciousness and intellectual elitism, recognizes that the clever and the powerful needed to sue for mercy, whereas the simple "come into their Kingdom".'

Hubert Doggart, *retired schoolmaster*

... to ensure sanity, there must be at least the elements of an internal disagreement ever present in a personality, and it is for that reason, ... that I address this attempt at an autobiography to you, dear me.

We were born in the normal manner in a London nursing-home, and here I must already give up the collective pronoun in case it be mistaken for *folie de grandeur* ... Grandeur there was, in a purely physical sense, although I hope not folie. I weighed nearly twelve pounds as a consequence of a reluctant and tardy birth ...

Of the events surrounding my birth I remember little, and must base my report on data from other sources. What I do know is that, whereas I was born in London (in a section ominously called Swiss Cottage), I was in fact conceived in Leningrad, in a tall, draughty and shell-pocked house ... It stands to reason that I travelled a great deal during the more than nine months which separated my conception in the shadow of revolution and political slogan, to my birth in the cold embrace of industrial smog and respectability, but once again my memory of the great social upheavals through which I passed disguised as a piece of overweight luggage can only be described as hazy, and therefore unreliable.

Peter Ustinov (1921–), from his autobiography *Dear Me*

'Peter Ustinov was my senior at Gibb's School, near Sloane Square, London. His writing seems effortlessly to combine knowledge and wisdom, humanity and humour. These paragraphs from *Dear Me* seem to me to support my claim!'

Rita Dove, *Commonwealth Professor of English, University of Virginia, and former US Poet Laureate*

For Sophie, Who'll be in First Grade in the Year 2000

No bright toy
this world we've left you.
Even the wrapping
is torn, the ribbons
grease-flecked and askew.
Still, it's all we have.

Wait a moment before
you pick it up. Study
its scratches, how it
shines in places. Now
love what you touch,
and you will touch wisely.

May the world, in your hands,
brighten with use. May you
sleep in sweet breath and
rise always in wonder
to mountain and forest,
greengaze and silk cheek –

dear Sophie,
littlest phoenix …

Rita Dove (1952–), from *On the Bus with Rosa Parks*

Sir Philip Dowson, *architect*

In his loneliness and fixedness he yearneth towards the journeying Moon, and the stars that still sojourn, yet still move onward; and everywhere the blue sky belongs to them, and is their appointed rest, and their native country and their own natural homes, which they enter unannounced, as lords that are certainly expected, and yet there is a silent joy at their arrival.

Samuel Taylor Coleridge (1772–1834)

'You ask, "Why?" As individuals, who are born and die alone, there is this place for wonder, discovery, hope, arrival, warmth and love'.

¶ This appears in the subtext margins of the 1817 edition of *The Ancient Mariner.*

Margaret Drabble, *author*

If you are going to refuse, do so at once.

Ann Dally

'This advice was given to me by Dr Ann Dally, friend and writer on medical matters and much else – a piece of wisdom I often invoke.'

Cecily Drummond, *artist and teacher*

⤿

To escape the distress caused by regret for the past or fear about the future, this is the rule to follow: leave the past to the infinite mercy of God, the future to His good providence; give the present wholly to His love by being faithful to His grace.

Jean-Pierre de Caussade (1675–1751), from 'The Providential Ordering of Life', *The Flame of Divine Love*

Ninette Dutton, *author and sheep farmer in south Australia*

⤿

Much Madness is Divinest Sense

Much Madness is divinest Sense –
To a discerning Eye –
Much Sense – the starkest Madness –
'Tis the Majority
In this, as All, prevail –
Assent – and you are sane –
Demur – you're straightway dangerous –
And handled with a Chain –

Emily Dickinson (1830–86), from *Collected Poems*

Juliet Dyer, *sculptor in clay*

⤿

Who *is* the Potter, pray, and who the Pot?

Edward Fitzgerald (1809–83), from *The Rubaiyat of Omar Khayyam*, stanza 88

'I interpreted this to my children as "who is the teacher and who the taught?" Or, "who is the maker, pray, and who the made?", there being the interaction between the active and the passive.'

James Dyson, *inventor*

⤳

Restlessness is discontent and discontent is the first necessity of progress. Show me a thoroughly satisfied man and I will show you a failure.

Thomas A. Edison (1847–1931)

HRH The Duke of Edinburgh

⤳

Since human beings, as well as other non-human sentient beings, depend upon the environment as the ultimate source of life and well-being, let us share the conviction that the conservation of the environment, the restoration of the imbalance caused by our negligence in the past, be implemented with courage and determination.

We are the generation with the awareness of a great danger. We are the ones with the responsibility and the ability to take steps of concrete action, before it is too late.

The Venerable Lungrig Namgyal Rinpoche (from the Buddhist Declaration on Nature to the interfaith ceremony at Assisi in 1986)

¶ The interfaith ceremony brought together the major religions and conservation groups. From this a new charity 'The Alliance of Religions and Conservation' (ARC) was formed under the guidance of HRH The Duke of Edinburgh. ARC now works with world religions in over 60 countries developing educational and practical projects to protect nature.

Hywel Teifi Edwards, *retired professor of Welsh, University of Wales*

The best education is that which … impresses the heart most with the love of virtue, which gives the deepest consciousness of the fallibility of the human understanding, which makes men diffident and modest, attentive to evidence, quick in discerning it, and determined to follow it; which, in short, instead of producing acute casuists, conceited pedants or furious polemicists, produces fair enquirers endowed with that heavenly wisdom described by Saint James, 'which is pure, then peaceable, gentle, easy to be entreated, full of mercy and good fruits, without partiality and without hypocrisy'. An education so conducted is the only means of gaining the progress of truth; of exterminating the pitiful prejudices we indulge against one another; and of establishing peace on earth and goodwill amongst men.

Dr Richard Price (1723–91)

Anita Emery, *dog breeder and dog-show judge*

You'll always have the memories,
Fond reminders of the love
That God has gladly welcomed
To His Kingdom up above;
And though they are in Heaven
In His comfort and His care,
Be thankful for the gift of life
And what you had to share.
Memories grow more precious still
When loved ones have to part
And remain forever blooming
In the gardens of the heart.

Anon.

Christopher Evans, *retired headmaster*

⤙

Cultivate simplicity

Charles Lamb (1775–1834), advice to Samuel Taylor Coleridge, 8 November 1796:

E'n la sua volontate é nostra pace …

'I translate this loosely as "In His Will is our peace …" '

Dante Alighieri (1265–1321), *La Divina Commedia* [*The Divine Comedy*],
Paradiso, canto iii, 85

The ewes which have not yet lambed, more than two hundred of them, wait in a hurdled space beyond the barn's open front, out of the wind but under no cover except the hard grey sky. The ground is thickly strawed. They are calm, unworried, but pack close together.

Sometimes it is difficult to tell, from the movements of the body under the wool, the precise moment when a lamb is born. The angle of the ewe's head, the curve and flexing of the neck as maternal licking starts, are the give-away. Then the mother is eased up on to her feet and follows her infant, carried ahead, into a pen of their own.

Just a ray of life, elongated like a fish, sodden, blood-smeared, collapsed. It is a moment we have all survived. I rub my hand up its length a time or two, jerking it towards existence. More rubs, a snuffled sneeze, and it breathes. The breath of life makes the rib cage swell and cave in unevenly until, after gasps and stutters, it holds a steady rhythm. Up comes the narrow, snake-like head, turning inquiringly this way and that as if the lamb, only two minutes 'old', had already mislaid something. The search is quickly over. It has found its mother's udder, and sucks. Milk begins to fill the tissues that were dehydrated for the journey into the light and air.

Out here, under the sky, the whiplash wind is as merciless as ever. But it has cleared the clouds. Overhead is a dome of stars, diamond-bright in the purity of empty night. Below them, and all around are clusters of light, earth's own constellations. To the south a red dot hangs low in the sky. It is the light on Salisbury Cathedral spire. The human race goes about its twentieth-century affairs. We have been back to the dawn of time.

Wilson Stephens, from A Year Observed

¶ In his book, Wilson Stephens, for many years editor of *The Field*, records with authority his own experience throughout twelve months of life and wildlife in rural Britain.

It is good to know the truth and to speak it. It is sometimes better to know the truth and to speak about palm trees.

Arab proverb, quoted by Nicholas Elliott in With My Little Eye

The Revd Meirion Evans, *Archdruid of Wales**

‿

Argument, again, is the death of conversation, if carried on in a spirit of hostility: but discussion is a pleasant and profitable thing …

… As a general rule, there is no conversation worth anything but between friends, or those who agree in the same leading views of a subject. Nothing was ever learnt by either side in a dispute. You contradict one another, will not allow a grain of sense in what your adversary advances, are blind to whatever makes against yourself, dare not look the question fairly in the face, so that you cannot avail yourself even of your real advantages, insist most on what you feel to be the weakest points of your argument, and get more and more absurd, dogmatical, and violent every moment. Disputes for victory generally end to the dissatisfaction of all parties; and the one recorded in Gil Blas breaks up just as it ought.

William Hazlitt (1778–1830), from The Plain Speaker

¶ * The Archdruid is the elected chief officer in the Gorsedd of Bards (allied to Wales's National Eisteddfod) and symbolic head of Welsh language and culture. The role bears no relationship to ancient druidism.

Tim Ffytche, *eye surgeon*

I am a part of all that I have met;
Yet all experience is an arch wherethro'
Gleams that untravell'd world, whose margin fades
For ever and for ever when I move.
How dull it is to pause, to make an end,
To rust unburnish'd, not to shine in use!

Alfred, Lord Tennyson (1809–92), from 'Ulysses'

We are the Pilgrims, master; we shall go
    Always a little further; it may be
Beyond that last blue mountain barred with snow,
    Across that angry or that glimmering sea,
White on a throne or guarded in a cave
    There lives a prophet who can understand
Why men were born …

James Elroy Flecker (1884–1915), from 'The Golden Journey to Samarkand',
v. 8, Epilogue

'Being more of a romantic than a realist, I have always found these verses very evocative, especially as my work in leprosy has taken me to remote places and introduced me to many creeds.'

Sir Ranulph Fiennes, *explorer*

⤳

Some dreams you have may seem unobtainable for a dozen different reasons, but don't be put off by all the apparent obstacles. The very act of starting the ball rolling will shift quite a few of them.

Matthew Fleming (1964–), *captain of Kent County Cricket Club*

⤳

It is better to try, and fail, than not to try at all.

Anon.

but

Always give yourself the best chance of success.

Anon.

Bill Fogarty, *Dublin postman*

⤳

Do good for yourselves by doing good for others.

Motto used by the St John of God's Christian Brothers in their homes for mentally handicapped people

¶ St John would leave his house at dusk, even if it were raining. Over his shoulder he would carry a large bag, and in one hand, two pots joined together with string. As he went through the streets of Granada, he shouted out 'Do good for yourselves, my brothers and sisters, do good for the love of God'.

Dr Hugo Ford, *oncologist*

Always do more than is expected of you, then you will never disappoint anyone.

General George Patton (1885–1945), US Army officer

Vicky Ford, *financier*

There is no such thing as a free lunch.

Frequently attributed to Milton Friedman, (1912–), US monetarist economist

¶ Professor Friedman often used this phrase, but his research traced it back at least as far as a notice in a nineteenth-century US tavern advertizing a free lunch for any patron buying a drink. The lunch was therefore hardly free.

Hendrika Foster, *retired physiotherapist and lecturer*

I commend
A level mind that grapples with what's here and now.
As for the rest, look on it as a river,
One moment calm and tame,
Gliding to meet the Tuscan Sea, the next
Churning, a chaos of gouged rocks, torn tree trunks
Corpses and rubble of houses,
While the mountains and forests amplify
The roar, and pitiless rain exacerbates
The temper of the water. Call him happy
And Lord of his own soul who every evening
Can say, 'Today I have lived.
Tomorrow Jove may blot the sky with cloud
Or fill it with pure sunshine, yet he cannot
Devalue what has once been held as precious,
Or tarnish or melt back
The gold the visiting hour has left behind.'

Horace (65–8 BC), *Odes*, 3. XXIX, trans. James Michie

Dick Francis, *author and retired jockey*

Don't despair if you make a right mess of a race. Everyone does, sometime. Just admit it to yourself. Never fool yourself. Don't get upset by criticism … and don't get swollen-headed from praise … and keep your temper at the races ALL the time. You can lose it as much as you like on the way home.

'This advice was given to me by my father when I started as an amateur jockey with the trainer George Owen in 1946. It is sound advice which I never forgot. I used it, word for word, in my novel *Bonecrack*, published in 1971.'

Lady Marion Fraser, *Chair of the Board of Christian Aid, 1990–97*

❧

Akok kan nesi keratami ayon.
[My stomach taught me.]

'A slim Turkana woman stood in the midst of her garden, created by eking out the meagre rainfall in the Laikipia region of Kenya. Her husband was disabled and the family had been compelled to leave their nomadic existence. Helped by our Kenyan partners, she had found this plot of land which she tended with her children, growing enough to feed themselves, with extra to sell in the local co-operative.

What struck me was the beauty of her garden, fenced against elephants, mixing, as it did, flowers with vegetables, fruit and grain, surrounded by shady trees.

"Who taught you to garden so imaginatively?" I asked.

I shall never forget her quiet reply,

"My stomach taught me."'

Dr Andrew Gailey, *schoolmaster*

 ↬

It is said that science will dehumanise people and turn them into numbers. That is false, tragically false. Look for yourself. This is the concentration camp and crematorium at Auschwitz. This is where people were turned into numbers. Into this pond were flushed the ashes of some four million people. And that was not done by gas. It was done by arrogance. It was done by dogma. It was done by ignorance. When people believe that they have absolute knowledge, with no test in reality, this is how they behave.

Science is a very human form of knowledge. We are always at the brink of the known. Every judgement in science stands on the edge of error. In the end the words were said by Oliver Cromwell: 'I beseech you, in the bowels of Christ, think it possible you may be mistaken.'

I owe it as a scientist and as a human being to the many members of my family who died at Auschwitz, to stand here by the pond as a survivor and a witness. We have to cure ourselves of the itch for absolute knowledge and power. We have to close the distance between the push-button order and the human act. We have to touch people.

Jacob Bronowski (1908–74), from *The Ascent of Man*

'The dangers of reducing people to numbers and of believing in "absolute truths" are as great as they have ever been. In the enormity of our modern world we still have to find ways "to touch people". Bumping into them doesn't count. We have to give up a little of ourselves to understanding them, to valuing others for themselves.'

Lesley Garrett, *opera singer*

 ↬

Spit on yer 'ands an' tek a fresh 'old.

'This saying was given to me by my mother, and I have used it throughout my life.'

Peter George, *friend*

A Happy to Accept Prayer for the Old

Most dear Lord
Now that
I am old
I think:
when you've lived
a long time
and experienced so much
people will respect you
and come to you
for help and guidance,
but sometimes
there are people
who think
you're a real
old fuddy-duddy
and that they
must be careful with you
in case you
talk too much
or fall over.
It's really comical
and often true
and so good
for us
when it happens.
Help me to laugh
and accept
and get on
with the joy
of living for You.

Rosa George (1907–88)

For it is the duty of the human understanding to understand that there are things which it cannot understand and what these things are.

Søren Kierkegaard (1813–55)

What, after all, is immortal fame? An empty hollow thing. To what then must we aspire? This, and this alone: the just thought, the unselfish act, the tongue that utters no falsehood, the temper that treats each passing event as something predestined, expected and emanating from the one source and origin.

Marcus Aurelius (121–80), from Meditations

Robert Gibson, *university emeritus professor*

Death is nothing at all. I have only slipped away into the next room. I am I and you are you. Whatever we were to each other we are still.

Call me by my old familiar name, speak to me in the easy way we always used. Put no difference in your tone; wear no forced air of solemnity or sorrow. Laugh as we always laughed at the little jokes together.

Play, smile, think of me, pray for me.

Let my name be ever the household word it was; let it be spoken without an effort, without a trace of shadow in it. Life means all that it ever meant; it is the same as it ever was; there is an absolutely unbroken continuity. What is this death but a negligible accident? Why should I be out of mind because I am out of sight? I am but waiting for you, for an interval, somewhere very near, just around the corner. All is well.

Canon Henry Scott Holland (1847–1918),
from a sermon preached on Whitsunday, 1910

I don't suppose there was any period in Herbert Farrant's life when he made a point of going to church with unfailing regularity. But I had a long relationship with him after his wife Minnie's death. He lived alone and I made a point of going to see him. For a long time we never talked about religion but eventually I suggested that he might care to have a blessing before I left. This became a regular feature of my visits.

On one occasion he'd been ill, but insisted he was better again. Then he said, 'I want to tell you something'; and proceeded to tell me that someone had been coming to his cottage in the night at about two o'clock … He called out 'Who's there?', but there was never any answer. He said, 'So I got me old gun out and I kep' it close by my bed. And the next time they come, I said 'Who's there?' and this time they said 'It's me!' D'you know who that was?' 'Yes,' I said, 'I know who it was.' He looked at me in some surprise and asked, 'Who was it, then?' 'It was Minnie,' I answered. He said, 'Yes … it was.'

… I visited him once more and I found that his 'sickness' was nothing else than that he'd had enough of life and was preparing to take his leave. I stood by his bed. He was weak but in no sort of pain. He said, 'Know where I'm goin'? I'm goin' *home*.' 'Yes,' I said, 'you are. I knew when you said that Minnie had come, that you might soon join her.' He died twenty-four hours later.

Revd Walter Lane (1908–88), Rector of Ashdon. From *Annals of Ashdon* 1988, collected by Robert Gibson

Josh Gifford, *race-horse trainer*

⤳

Always be polite. It costs nothing, people like it and it does nothing but good.

'My first boss's advice to me.'

Air Chief Marshal Sir John Gingell,
Gentleman Usher of the Black Rod

For everything there is a season, and a time for every matter under heaven:

a time to be born, and a time to die;
a time to plant, and a time to pluck up what is planted;
a time to kill, and a time to heal;
a time to break down, and a time to build up;
a time to weep, and a time to laugh;
a time to mourn, and a time to dance;
a time to cast away stones, and a time to gather stones together;
a time to embrace, and a time to refrain from embracing;
a time to seek, and a time to lose;
a time to keep, and a time to cast away;
a time to rend, and a time to sew;
a time to keep silence, and a time to speak;
a time to love, and a time to hate;
a time for war, and a time for peace.
What gain has the worker from his toil?
I have seen the business that God has given to the sons of men to be busy with.

He has made everything beautiful in its time; also he has put eternity into man's mind, yet so that he cannot find out what God has done from the beginning to the end.

Ecclesiastes 3: I–XI (RSV)

The Bulwark

Strange is the Vigour in a Brave Man's Soul. The strength of his Spirit and his irresistible Power, the Greatness of his Heart and Height of his Condition, his mighty Confidence and Contempt of Dangers, his true Security and Repose in himself, his Liberty to dare and do what he pleaseth, his Alacrity in the midst of Fears, his invincible Temper, are advantages which make him Master of Fortune. His Courage fits him for all Attempts, renders him serviceable to GOD and MAN, and makes him the Bulwark and Defence of his King and Country.

Thomas Traherne (1637–74)

'This was quoted in *The Times* on the occasion of the death of Sir Winston Churchill.'

Victoria Glendinning, *writer*

↬

The ant's a centaur in his dragon world.
Pull down thy vanity, it is not man
Made courage, or made order, or made grace.
       Pull down thy vanity, I say pull down.
Learn of the green world what can be thy place
In scaled invention or true artistry,
       Pull down thy vanity …
Rathe* to destroy, niggard in charity,
Pull down thy vanity,
       I say pull down.

But to have done instead of not doing
       this is not vanity.
To have gathered from the air a live tradition
Or from a fine old eye the unconquered flame
This is not vanity.
       Here error is all in the not done,
All in the diffidence that faltered.

Ezra Pound (1885–1972), from *The Pisan Cantos*

*Rathe, quick or prompt

Nothing is forever.

'I have this pinned up and it reminds me that bad times will come to an end and good times cannot be taken for granted.'

Graeme R. Goldsworthy, *Director, International Demining Group*

⌒

Look from the viewpoint of the heart and contradictions will start melting like ice.

Guru Bagwam Shree Rajneesh (d. 1990)

'In May 2001 a widow lost three of her four children to an explosive device. Apart from the trauma and the grief, her poverty was so acute that she could not afford coffins and had laid their bodies out on the bed. Local villagers clubbed together to pay for the funeral. This happened in El Salvador, a supposedly "mine-free" country. It was through looking into hearts, not heads, that the opposing groups in El Salvador finally agreed on a way of recognizing and tackling the problem of a land contaminated with unexploded mines and bombs.'

❡ Graeme has worked on mine-clearance since 1993. He now runs a team of volunteer mine-clearance workers.

Talking about the techniques involved, he quoted Wellington's advice, 'Reconnaissance is nine-tenths of the battle' and explains that when working on a mine or bomb you must try to understand the mind of the constructor and always be prepared for the unexpected.

Sir Nicholas Goodison, *banker and author*

⌒

I beseech you, in the bowels of Christ, think it possible you may be mistaken.

Oliver Cromwell (1599–1658), in a letter to the Church of Scotland, 3 August 1650

The first list we made out had to be discarded. It was clear that the upper reaches of the Thames would not allow of the navigation of a boat sufficiently large to take the things we had set down as indispensable; so we tore the list up, and looked at one another.

George said:

'You know we are on the wrong track altogether. We must not think of the things we could do with, but only of the things that we can't do without.'

George comes out really quite sensible at times. You'd be surprised. I call that downright wisdom, not merely as regards the present case, but with reference to our trip up the river of life generally. How many people, on that voyage, load up the boat till it is ever in danger of swamping with a store of foolish things which they think essential to the pleasure and comfort of the trip, but which are really only useless lumber.

How they pile the poor little craft mast-high with fine clothes and big houses … with formalities and fashions, with pretence and ostentation, and with – oh, heaviest, maddest lumber of all! – the dread of what will my neighbour think …

… Throw it overboard! … It makes [the boat] so cumbersome and dangerous to manage, you never gain a moment's rest for dreamy laziness – no time to watch the windy shadows … or the great trees by the margin looking down at their own image …

… Let your boat of life be light, packed with only what you need – a homely home and simple pleasures, one or two friends, worth the name, someone to love and someone to love you, a cat, a dog, and a pipe or two …

… You will have time to think as well as to work. Time to drink in life's sunshine …

I beg your pardon, really. I quite forgot.

Well, we left the list to George, and he began it.

Jerome K. Jerome (1859–1927), from *Three Men in a Boat*

Pat Graham, *teacher and guide at the Royal Albatross Colony, Dunedin, New Zealand*

Te manu e kai i te miro nona te ngahere.
Te manu e kai i te matauranga nona te ao.

[The bird that feeds on the miro berry has the bush as its domain.
The bird that feeds from learning has the world as its domain.]

Traditional Maori saying

'There are about 10,000 albatross in the colony, but they spend most of their time at sea. It takes them one year to rear a chick and the following year to recover from the effort.'

Julia Green, *drug-addiction counsellor*

One puff is a thousand too many and a thousand is never enough.

'A crack cocaine addict told me this. If only a few of the addicts I see are cured, then I must think of the potential victims of crime saved. Addicts may need up to £1000 per day to feed their craving. Alcoholics Anonymous has a similar saying.'

Baroness Greenfield, *neuroscientist*

It is often true that only by going too far can we find out how far we can go.

T. S. Eliot (1888–1965), in his 1942 lecture 'The Music of Poetry', from *On Poetry and Poets*

It is better to light a candle than to curse the darkness.

Chinese proverb

John Gresswell, *retired farmer*

⌐

And another thing. Love is temporary madness, it erupts like volcanoes and then subsides. And when it subsides you have to make a decision. You have to work out whether your roots have so entwined together that it is inconceivable that you should ever part. Because this is what love is. Love is not breathlessness, it is not excitement, it is not the promulgation of promises of eternal passion, it is not the desire to mate every second minute of the day, it is not lying awake at night imagining that he is kissing every cranny of your body. That is just being 'in love', which any fool can do. Love itself is what is left over when being in love has burned away, and this is both an art and a fortunate accident. Your mother and I had it, we had roots that grew towards each other underground, and when all the pretty blossom had fallen from our branches we found that we were one tree and not two.

Louis de Bernières (1954–), from *Captain Corelli's Mandolin*

Tanni Grey-Thompson, *paralympic gold medal athlete*

⌐

Aim high – even if you hit a cabbage!

'One of the best pieces of advice that I received from my grandfather. It was a favourite of his and helped me through my athletic career and life. If you don't aim high you never know what you might achieve nor the limits you can push yourself to.'

Richard Griffiths, *actor*

⤳

A great warrior who had lived with honour and truthfulness died and was greeted by a gatekeeper of Heaven, who was to be his guide.

He was taken at once to a gigantic banqueting hall and saw that everyone sat at long tables laden with the finest food imaginable. The most peculiar aspect of the feast was the chopsticks. These were five feet long and made of silver and teak. The warrior asked his guide about them, because it was impossible to eat with them.

'Ah yes,' said the guide, 'But see how we do things in Heaven.' The warrior turned and saw that all the banqueters were using the chopsticks to feed the person sitting opposite.

Later the warrior, being deeply curious, asked his guide if he might be given a glimpse of Hell.

'Of course,' said the guide, and led him back into the banqueting hall they had just left. When the warrior pointed this out the guide replied, 'To look at, Hell is no different from Heaven.' The multitudes sat, as before, at tables groaning with the finest foods. The warrior was confused. It seemed exactly the same as Heaven. 'Observe,' said the guide, 'No one can trust his neighbour.' The warrior saw that the people with their long chopsticks were trying only to feed themselves, and thus, amidst plenty, they starved.

Buddhist story

❡ This story is often told at O Ben services held in August to commemorate the lives of those who have died during the previous year. It may have originated from Korea or Japan and has many different wordings. There is also a similar story in Jewish tradition.

General Lord Guthrie of Craigiebank, *former Chief of Defence Staff*

⌒

If you want to become a general, never get separated from your kit, never march on Moscow and never enter the Balkans.

Military wisdom

'This is some advice/wisdom we received at Sandhurst.'

Sir Ernest Hall, *pianist and entrepreneur*

⌒

The only failure is to give up trying.

'This simple sentence ensures that you never become the victim of circumstance.'

Sir Peter Hall, *director and producer*

⌒

What is wrong is not, of course, the great discoveries of science – information is always better than ignorance. What is wrong is the belief behind the information, the belief that information alone will change the world. It won't. Information without human understanding is like an answer without its question … meaningless. And human understanding is only possible through the arts. It is the work of art that creates the human perspective in which information turns to truth. Without those last quartets of Beethoven, without *Oedipus the King*, without a *Hamlet* or a *Lear* or Michelangelo's ceiling or the Odes of Keats, the electronic age could be a nightmare – a brighter, louder more disastrous nightmare than any that has gone before. With the arts, it could become a great, perhaps the greatest, age.

Attributed to Archibald Macleish (1892–1982)

❡ The source could not be found but Macleish's literary executor Richard McAdoo agrees that this sounds like his voice in both style and substance.

Lady Hallifax, *President of the Motor Neurone Disease Association*

⌒

Look backwards with gratitude.
Look forward with hope.
Look upward with confidence.

'This helped me enormously after my husband's death. I keep it by the bathroom mirror and think of it often.'

❡ Admiral Hallifax had a key role during the Falklands War. He died from motor neurone disease, which he fought with great courage. Anne works unstintingly for the Motor Neurone Disease Association.

Robin Heath, *Professor of Dentistry*

Yᴏᴜ can get anything done if you don't want the credit.

O. V. S. Heath (1903–97), plant physiologist

'An aphorism of my father's, said of effecting change in universities but widely true.'

Paddy Heazell, *retired headmaster*

… Yᴏᴜ and I are old;
Old age hath yet his honour and his toil;
Death closes all: but something ere the end,
Some work of noble note may yet be done …
Come, my friends …
Push off, and sitting well in order smite
The sounding furrows; for my purpose holds
To sail beyond the sunset, and the paths
Of all the western stars, until I die …
Tho' much is taken, much abides and tho'
We are not now that strength which in old days
Moved earth and heaven; that which we are, we are;
One equal temper of heroic hearts,
Made weak by time and fate, but strong in will
To strive, to seek, to find, and not to yield.

Alfred, Lord Tennyson (1809–92), from 'Ulysses'

Paul Heim, *barrister*

⌇

'If each party to a marriage puts in more than they expect to get out, then each party will get out more than they put in.'

Robert Hobhouse, *teacher*

⌇

'Goodbye,' said the fox, 'And now here is my secret, a very simple secret: It is only with the heart that one can see rightly; what is essential is invisible to the eye.'

'What is essential is invisible to the eye,' the little prince repeated, so that he would be sure to remember.

'It is the time you have wasted for your rose that makes your rose so important.'

'It is the time I have wasted for my rose' said the little prince, so that he would be sure to remember.

'Men have forgotten this truth,' said the fox. 'But you must not forget it. You become responsible, forever, for what you have tamed. You are responsible for the rose …'

'I am responsible for my rose,' the little prince repeated, so that he would be sure to remember.

Antoine de Saint-Exupéry (1900–44), from *The Little Prince*

Michael Holroyd, *author*

⤜

The last word in wisdom is not to desire disciples but to keep friends.

Hugh Kingsmill (1889–1949)

A charlatan makes obscure what is clear, a thinker makes clear what is obscure.

Hugh Kingsmill (1889–1949)

¶ From Michael Holroyd, *The Best of Hugh Kingsmill*

Dr Mererid Hopwood, *poet and winner of Chair for Poetry, National Eisteddfod of Wales 2001*

⤜

Das Wiedersehen

Ein Mann der Herrn K. lange nicht gesehen hatte, begrüsste ihn mit den Worten: 'Sie haben sicht gar nicht verändert.' 'Oh!' sagte Herr K., und erbleichte.

[*The Reunion*

A man, whom Mr K. had not seen for years, greeted him with the words: 'You haven't changed a bit.' 'Oh!' said Mr K., and turned pale.]

Bertolt Brecht (1898–1956), from *Kalendergeschichten*

'I have become increasingly aware of the "truth" in this anecdote or micro-story. The wisdom to change, to learn from life as one grows older, is a precious gift indeed!'

Sheelah Horsfield, *gardener*

Y͏ou learn from experience. A man never wakes his second child just to see him smile.

Mark Twain (1835–1910)

Lady Innes of Edingight, *prison visitor*

'F͏ather Rodriguez was one of the thousands of Christians tortured and put to death in Japan during the seventeenth century. In prison, unable to pray and listening to the indifferent laughter and chatter of the guards, Endo writes that Rodriguez reflected as follows.'

"Sin is not what it is usually thought to be; it is not to steal and tell lies. Sin is for one man to walk brutally over the life of another and to be quite oblivious of the wounds he has left behind." And then for the first time a real prayer rose up in his heart.

Shusaku Endo, (1923–96), from *Silence*

Lucinda Jackson, *philosophy teacher*

W͏ithout beginning, middle or end, of infinite power,
of infinite arms, whose eyes are the moon and sun,
I see thee, whose face is flaming fire,
Burning this whole universe with Thy radiance.

Bhagavad Gita, IX: verse 19, trans. Franklin Edgerton (1885–1963)

Sir Derek Jacobi, *actor*

There's a special providence in the fall of a sparrow. If it be now, 'tis not to come; if it be not to come, it will be now; if it be not now, yet it will come: The readiness is all.

William Shakespeare (1564–1616), from *Hamlet,* Act V, Scene ii

❡ Sir Derek underlined 'The readiness is all'. Was Hamlet referring to the sparrow in Luke 12: 4–7? If so, verse 5 has a terrible resonance in the light of the action to follow.

I tell you, my friends, do not fear
those who kill the body, and after that
have no more that they can do.
    But I will warn you whom to fear: fear him who,
after he has killed, has power to cast into
hell; yes, I tell you, fear him!
    Are not five sparrows sold for two pennies? And
not one of them is forgotten before God.
    Why, even the hairs of your head are all
numbered. Fear not; you are of more
value than many sparrows.

Luke 12: 4–7 (RSV)

Francis Jacobs, *advocate-general, European Court of Justice*

꘏

Pâté de Vie

Take two young people.
Do not separate them.
Place them in a dwelling and add:
> 2 large measures each of good temper, patience,
> understanding, thoughtfulness,
> tolerance and laughter.

Then add:
> measure of tidiness
> measure of ambition

and a good sprinkling of discussion.

Mix all together with an
equal quantity of love
and let it stand.

If too much spice has been
added, the mixture may curdle.
If so, add another measure
of understanding and tolerance
and more love, and then the
mixture will become smooth.

Watch carefully. Curdling must
NEVER be allowed to continue
overnight. This would endanger the whole.

Now moisten the whole thoroughly
with the milk of human kindness
mixed with equal parts of common
sense and laughter. Strain to
remove any sarcasm, bitterness
or jealousy. Then sprinkle liberally
with a sense of humour.

Cook gently in the love of God
over the fire of knowledge and wisdom.

The Pâté is now ready.

At intervals stir in pinches of
relatives and friends. These
contribute greatly to the spicy taste.

If this recipe is followed carefully
the Pâté will last a lifetime and
flavour will increase over the years.

NEVER put it in the deep freeze or refrigerator.

Attributed to Dorothy Lindsay (*c.* 1890–1980), grandmother of a large family.

'Given to us on the occasion of our marriage in 1975 by Dorothy Lindsay.'

Canon Eric James, *Extra Chaplain to Her Majesty The Queen*

⬱

Charity is the careful enquiry into the needs of one's fellow men
that enables one to give the exact help needed.

Charles Freer Andrews (1871–1940)

'As Director of Christian Action for over ten years I have found this quotation very useful.

Charles Freer Andrews' feeling for South London, where he was warden
of a Walworth mission, is recorded in his book, *What I Owe to Christ*. In
1904 he joined the staff of St Stephen's College, Delhi. When in South Africa
in 1914 he met Gandhi, with whom he maintained a lasting friendship.'

Baroness James of Holland Park (P. D. James), *author*

⤳

Almighty God, the fountain of all wisdom, who knowest our necessities before we ask, and our ignorance in asking; We beseech thee to have compassion upon our infirmities; and those things, which for our unworthiness we dare not, and for our blindness cannot ask, vouchsafe to give us, for the worthiness of thy Son Jesus Christ our Lord. Amen.

Book of Common Prayer, collect following Holy Communion

Rt Revd Penny Jamieson, *Bishop of Dunedin, New Zealand*

⤳

Batter my Heart, Three-person'd God; For, You

Batter my heart, three-person'd God; for, you
As yet but knock, breathe, shine, and seek to mend;
That I may rise and stand, o'erthrow me, and bend
Your force to break, blow, burn, and make me new.
I, like an usurp'd town to another due,
Labour to admit you, but oh, to no end;
Reason, your viceroy in me, me should defend,
But is captiv'd, and proves weak or untrue.
Yet dearly I love you, and would be lov'd fain,
But am betroth'd unto your enemy;
Divorce me, untie or break that knot again,
Take me to you, imprison me, for I,
Except you' enthrall me, never shall be free,
Nor ever chaste, except you ravish me.

John Donne (1572–1631)

Sir Antony Jay, *scriptwriter and author*

People of the same trade seldom meet together, even for merriment and diversion, but the conversation ends in a conspiracy against the public, or in some contrivance to raise prices.

Adam Smith (1723–90), from *The Wealth of Nations*, Vol. 2, Book 1, Chapter 10

Because half a dozen grasshoppers under a fern make the field ring with their importunate chink, while thousands of great cattle, reposed beneath the shadow of the British oak, chew the cud and are silent, pray do not imagine that those who make the noise are the only inhabitants of the field.

Edmund Burke (1729–97), from *Reflections on the Revolution in France*

Simon Jenkins, *writer and columnist*

As good almost kill a man as kill a good book: who kills a man kills a reasonable creature, God's image; but he who destroys a good book, kills reason itself, kills the image of God, as it were, in the eye.

A good book is the precious life-blood of a master spirit, embalmed and treasured up on purpose to a life beyond life.

John Milton (1608–74), from *Aeropagitica*, published 1644

Flora Johnson, *schoolgirl, primary school reception class*

☙

On visiting a hospital ward:

Ben (aged two): 'Mummy can we jump on the beds?'
Flora (aged four): 'No Ben, only the nurses are allowed to jump on the beds.'

Crossing the Somerset moors on a misty morning:

Flora: 'God made it beautiful.'

Sir John Johnson, *diplomat, conservationist and walker, Chairman of the Countryside Commission*

☙

Stonehenge, Friday, 27 August 1875

Today I paid my first visit to Stonehenge.

We had breakfast before Church and immediately afterwards Morris and I started to walk to Stonehenge, eleven miles.

Passing through Salisbury and the beautiful Cathedral Close we took the Devizes road and after some six miles saw in the dim distance the mysterious Stones standing upon the Plain. We pushed on to the clump of trees which shelters the Druid's Head Inn from the S.W. winds and had a merry luncheon, then struck across the Plain towards the Stones.

The sun was hot, but a sweet, soft air moved over the Plain 'wafting' the scent of the purple heather tufts and the beds of thyme and making the delicate blue harebells tremble on their fragile stems. A wheatear flitted before us from one stone heap to another along the side of the wheel track … Around us the Plain heaved mournfully with great and solemn barrows … It seemed to be holy ground and the very Acre of God. Beyond Ambresbury [*sic*] the Plain swelled into bolder hills, and dark clumps of trees here and there marked the crests and high places of the downs, while the white and dusty road glared away northwards across the great undulations of the rolling Plain.

[As we crossed] the turf eastward we came in sight of the grey cluster of gigantic Stones ... It seemed to me as if they were ancient giants stiffened into stone who might at any moment come alive ...

It is a solemn, awful place. As I entered the charmed circle I uncovered my head. It was like entering a great Cathedral. A silent service was going on and the Stones whispered to each other the grand secret. The Sun was present at the service in his Temple and the place was filled with his glory. We sat under the shadow of the great leaning stone upon the vast monolith which has fallen upon, and crushed, the Hearth or Altar Stone.

[Later, as we descended] the southern slope of the Plain, we left the Stones standing against the sky, seeming by turns to be the Giants, the Preachers, the Watchers, the Cathedral on the Plain.

Revd Francis Kilvert (1793–1863), from his *Diary*

Dr Lucy Johnson, *geriatrician*

Injustice, poverty, slavery, ignorance – these may be cured by reform or revolution. But men do not live only by fighting evils. They live by positive goals, individual and collective, a vast variety of them, seldom predictable, at times incompatible.

Isaiah Berlin (1909-97), from *Political Ideas in the Twentieth Century*

The Rt Revd and Rt Hon. Nöel Jones,
Bishop of Sodor and Man

~

The Nothing People

They do not lie;
They just neglect to tell the truth.
They do not take;
They simply cannot bring themselves to give.
They will not rock the boat;
But did you ever see them pull an oar? …
They do not hurt you;
They merely will not help you.
They do not hate you;
They merely cannot love you.
They will not burn you;
They'll only fiddle while you burn.
They are the nothing people;
The sins-of-omission folk;
So give me every time an
honest sinner, or even a Saint.
[But] protect me from the
nothing people.

Anon.

Tim Kirkbride, *retired company director*

⤳

Prayer for Friends

God, who has given us the love of women
and the friendship of men, keep alive in
our hearts the sense of old fellowship and
tenderness, make offences to be forgotten
and services to be remembered; protect those
whom we love in all things and follow them
with kindness, so that they may lead simple
and unsuffering lives, and in the end die
easily with quiet minds.

Robert Louis Stevenson (1850–94), from *Travels with a Donkey in the Cevennes*

We shall not cease from exploration
And the end of all our exploring
Will be to arrive where we started
And know the place for the first time.
Through the unknown, remembered gate
When the last of earth left to discover
Is that which was the beginning;
At the source of the longest river
The voice of the hidden waterfall
And the children in the apple-tree
Not known, because not looked for
But heard, half-heard, in the stillness
Between two waves of the sea.
Quick now, here, now, always –
A condition of complete simplicity
(Costing not less than everything)
And all shall be well and
All manner of thing shall be well
When the tongues of flame are in-folded
Into the crowned knot of fire
And the fire and the rose are one.

T. S. Eliot (1888–1965), from 'Little Gidding', *Four Quartets*

Sir Robin Knox-Johnston, *master mariner*

'The most valuable item to take with you to sea is a healthy dose of apprehension.'

Henry Lang, *farmer and countryman*

And he gave it of his opinion, that whoever could make two ears of corn or two blades of grass grow upon a spot of ground where only one grew before, would deserve better of mankind, and do more essential service to his country than the whole race of politicians put together.

Jonathan Swift (1667–1745), from *Gulliver's Travels*

'As a farmer I often reflect on how many are still hungry in the world.'

Admiral Sir Michael Layard

Abou Ben Adhem (may his tribe increase!)
Awoke one night from a dream of peace,
And saw, within the moonlight in his room,
Making it rich, and like a lily in bloom,
An angel writing in a book of gold:–
Exceeding peace had made Ben Adhem bold,
And to the presence in the room he said,
'What writest thou?' – The vision raised its head,
And with a look made of all sweet accord,
Answered, 'The names of those who love the Lord.'
'And is mine one?' said Abou. 'Nay, not so,'
Replied the angel. Abou spoke more low,
But cheerly still; and said, 'I pray thee, then,
Write me as one who loves his fellow men.'
The angel wrote, and vanished. The next night
It came again with a great wakening light,
And showed the names whom love of God had blest,
And lo! Ben Adhem's name led all the rest.

James Henry Leigh Hunt (1784–1859)

Hugh Leach, *retired diplomat*

Money lost, nothing lost.
Health lost, much lost.
Honour lost, all lost.

Arab saying

'I first heard this from an old Bedouin when I went to Arabia over 40 years ago. I have dwelled on its wisdom ever since.'

Remember the kettle, always in hot water yet always singing.

Anon.

'Worth remembering when one is in trouble.'

John Leach, *third-generation potter*

The wise man is he who, in his maturity, uses the natural gifts with which he was born.

Attributed to Confucius (551–479 BC)

'This was often quoted by my grandfather, Bernard Leach, CH.

In his youth he was teaching copperplate engraving in Japan, when he met a group of philosophers at a Japanese tea ceremony. He joined their discussions and they presented him with a ceramic pot to decorate. He understood, from that moment, that ceramics have an intrinsic value and beauty. He later became the seventh Kenzan in a line of master-potters.'

¶ John Leach's pottery lies near the abbey ruins at Muchelney in Somerset. He has handed on his skills to many, and on open days may be found surrounded by children watching pots take shape on the wheel.

Walter J. Leach, *stained-glass artist (aged 102)*

‿

When you look at other people's work try to see what is good in it. They will have something to offer.

'As a lad I was apprenticed to the popular Victorian stained-glass artist Henry Victor Milner, and this was his advice to me. I would spend my two-week annual holiday going by bicycle to see our recent work *in situ* and would put his advice into practice. I learned a lot that way. I worked with Milner for 24 years. Our biggest commission, the windows in York's Guildhall, finished up in a molten state, flowing to the ground after a German incendiary bomb raid in 1946, but the windows in Dunnington Church, York, and many others are still in place.'

The Hon. Barnabas Leith, *Secretary-General, Baha'i Community, UK*

‿

The Hidden Words

O Children of Men!
    Know ye not why We created you from the same dust? That no one should exalt himself over the other. Ponder at all times in your hearts how ye were created. Since We have created you all from the one same substance it is incumbent on you to be even as one soul, to walk with the same feet, eat with the same mouth and dwell in the same land, that from your inmost being, by your deeds and actions, the signs of oneness and the essence of detachment may be made manifest.

Baha'u'llah

'I strive to live by this day by day.'

Clare Libby, *typesetter*

⮌

That the birds of worry and care fly above your head, this you cannot help; that they nest in your hair, this you can avoid. (Anon)

Gary Lineker, *footballer and sports commentator*

⮌

Circumstances do not determine a man, they reveal him.

James Allen* (1849–1925)

¶ *Author and writer of short stories from Kentucky.

Julian Litchfield, *publican*

⮌

It's a great art in life to be able to speak, but an even greater one is to know when to be quiet.

'Some words of wisdom from my father. He was a daily pub-goer and now, as a publican, his words frequently come to me as I look at the crowds around my bar!'

Sister Helen Loder, *priest and leader of St Saviour's Priory Community*

Send forth wisdom from the holy heavens,
and from the throne of your glory send her,
that she may labour at my side,
and that I may learn what is pleasing to you.

Wisdom of Solomon 9: 10, Apocrypha (NRSV)

❡ St Saviour's Anglican Community in East London works through prayer and practical help for the homeless and others who are suffering.

John Lonergan, *Governor of Mountjoy Prison, Dublin*

There but for Fortune

Show me the prison, show me the jail,
Show me the prisoner whose life has gone stale,
And I'll show you, young man, with so many reasons why,
There but for fortune go you or I.

Show me the alley, show me the train,
Show me the hobo who sleeps out in the rain,
And I'll show you, young man, with so many reasons why,
There but for fortune go you or I.

Show me the whiskey stains on the floor,
Show me the drunkard as he stumbles out the door,
And I'll show you, young man, with so many reasons why,
There but for fortune go you or I.

Show me the country where the bombs had to fall,
Show me the ruins of the buildings once so tall,
And I'll show you, young man, with so many reasons why,
There but for fortune go you or I.

Phil Ochs (1940–97)

'I find this profound and challenging and use it often in talks.'

❡ Phil Ochs was born in El Paso, Texas. A passionate protest song-writer and contemporary of Bob Dylan and Joan Baez, he took his own life in 1976.

Sir Bernard Lovell, *Professor of Radioastronomy, founder and Director of Jodrell Bank Observatory*

Now faith is the substance of things
hoped for, the evidence of things not seen.

Hebrews 11: 1 (AV)

'In my later years, I think about this wonderful piece about faith whenever I listen to young theorists.'

'M', *refugee granted asylum*

Dust mashomar an ke dar ne'mat zanad
Laf e Yari va baradar khwandegi
Dust an bashad keh girad dast e dust
Dar parishan hali va darmandegi.

[Do not take as a friend the man who tells you constantly that he is your friend but take as your friend the man who takes your hand when you are down.]

'I learned this from my father.'

Sir Donald Maitland, *former diplomat*

~

… what doth the Lord require of thee but to do justly, and to love mercy, and to walk humbly with thy God.

Micah 6: 8 (AV)

In the green hills on the North-East frontier [at Kohima] there is a monument to those who died when the Japanese advance into India was halted in 1944 and the tide of the war in Burma turned. It bears a message on behalf of those it honours:

> 'When you go home, tell them of us and say
> *For your tomorrow we gave our today.*'

As the years passed in enjoyment of the blessings of this life, I thought more and more of the friends of my youth who had also left home to go to war but had not returned. I was more than ever persuaded, as I know were many of my contemporaries, that devoting my today and my tomorrow to the service of the public good was the best way in which I could hope to make their sacrifice worthwhile.

Donald Maitland (1922–), from *Diverse Times, Sundry Places*

❡ Sir Donald has been involved in public service from 1947 to the present time, notably as UK representative to the UN and then to the EEC.

The Rt Hon. John Major, *former prime minister*

~

Never forget the other man has a point of view too – and he may be right.

Abraham Thomas Major to his son, John, as a boy

Anthony Marreco, *barrister and publisher*

⌐

There are only two kinds of fool in this world. Those who give advice and those who don't take it.

'This advice was given to me by an old friend, Pat Herdman, whose family still manufacture linen in County Tyrone.'

Sir Clive Martin, *Lord Mayor of London, 1999–2000*

⌐

If

If you can keep your head when all about you
    Are losing theirs and blaming it on you;
If you can trust yourself when all men doubt you,
    But make allowance for their doubting too;
If you can wait and not be tired by waiting,
    Or being lied about, don't deal in lies,
Or being hated, don't give way to hating,
    And yet don't look too good, nor talk too wise.

  …

If you can fill the unforgiving minute
    With sixty seconds' worth of distance run,
Yours is the Earth and everything that's in it,
    And – which is more – you'll be a Man, my son!

Rudyard Kipling (1865–1936)

Robert Maxwell Wood, *artist and tutor*

I am returning to the ideas I had in the country before I knew the Impressionists ... Instead of trying to reproduce exactly what I have before my eyes, I use colour more arbitrarily so as to express myself forcibly ...

I should like to paint the portrait of an artist friend, a man who dreams great dreams, who works as the nightingale sings, because it is his nature. He'll be a fair man. I want to put into the picture my appreciation, the love that I have for him. So I paint him as he is, as faithfully as I can, to begin with.

But the picture is not finished yet. To finish it I am now going to be the arbitrary colourist. I exaggerate the fairness of the hair, I get to orange tones, chromes and pale lemon yellow.

Beyond the head, instead of painting the ordinary wall of the mean room, I paint infinity, a plain background of the richest, intensest blue that I can contrive, and by this simple combination the bright head illuminated against a rich blue background acquires a mysterious effect, like a star in the depths of an azure sky.

Vincent Van Gogh (1853–90), in a letter to his brother Theo, August 1888

¶ Vincent Van Gogh did not sell a single painting during his life. He could not have survived as an artist without the support of his brother, Theo, himself an art-dealer.

Sir Trevor McDonald, *broadcaster*

I think continually of those who were truly great.
Who, from the womb, remembered the soul's history
Through corridors of light where the hours are suns,
Endless and singing. Whose lovely ambition
Was that their lips, still touched with fire,
Should tell of the Spirit, clothed from head to foot in song.
And who hoarded from the Spring branches
The desires falling across their bodies like blossoms.

What is precious, is never to forget
The essential delight of the blood drawn from ageless springs
Breaking through rocks in worlds before our earth.
Never to deny its pleasure in the morning simple light
Nor its grave evening demand for love.
Never to allow gradually the traffic to smother
With noise and fog, the flowering of the Spirit.

Near the snow, near the sun, in the highest fields,
See how these names are fêted by the waving grass
And by the streamers of white cloud
And whispers of wind in the listening sky.
The names of those who in their lives fought for life,
Who wore at their hearts the fire's centre.
Born of the sun, they travelled a short while toward the sun
And left the vivid air signed with their honour.

Stephen Spender (1909–95)

Roger McGough, *poet*

⌒

The difference between someone who loves
And someone who hates,
Is that someone who hates
Has to explain what he means.

Roger McGough (1937–), from '10.15 Thursday Morning, Memphis, Tennessee'

Margaret McQueen, *retired head teacher*

⌒

We all of us try to make God in our image. It is one of our worst
temptations.

High Hills

There is much comfort in high hills
and a great easing of the heart.
We look upon them and our nature fills
with loftier images from their life apart.
They set our feet on curves of freedom, bent
to shape the circles of our discontent.

G. W. Young (1876–1958)

❡ Geoffrey Winthrop Young was a poet and a mountaineer who climbed
despite having only one leg.

Norris McWhirter, *co-founder of* Guinness Book of Records *and Olympic commentator*

N ever forget that if a man cons his wife he may also con you.

Jack Crump

'Coming in a plane back from Sweden I sat next to Jack Crump OBE, team manager for the British Olympics, 1948–72. He gave me this piece of wisdom which I have never forgotten.'

Captain Richard Meryon, *officer, Royal Navy*

B ut from the beginning of the creation God made them male and female.

For this cause shall a man leave his father and mother, and cleave to his wife;

And they twain shall be one flesh: so then they are no more twain, but one flesh.

What therefore God hath joined together, let not man put asunder.

Mark 10: 6–9 (AV)

Cliff Michelmore, *retired broadcaster*

Light and colour, freedom and delicious air give exquisite pleasure to the senses; but the heart searches deeper, and draws forth food for itself from sunshine, hills and sea, desiring beauty so deeply. That desire is a thirst which slakes itself to grow stronger. It springs afresh from the light, from the blue-hill yonder, from the gorse-flower at hand; to seize upon something which they symbolise; to absorb it and feel conscious of it – a something that cannot be defined, but which corresponds with all that is highest, truest and most ideal within the mind.

Richard Jefferies (1848–87), from his essay 'On the Downs (Hills and Vale)', first published in the *Standard*, May 1833

'Grieving needs time and space, peace and, above all, patience. I found this passage very helpful at a time of grief.'

Richenda Miers, *writer*

When the Good Lord made time, He made plenty of it.

Said by Roderick Steele, a crofter from South Uist

Shazia Mirza, *stand-up comic*

⤔

Listen to you. Nobody knows you better than yourself. Except God. If you hear Him, listen to Him and forget about the voices in your head!

'My mum gave me this advice.'

¶ Shazia Mirza, school clown, teacher, biochemist, stand-up comic and devout Muslim has said that she is excited about her wedding because she can't wait to meet her husband.

Adrian Mitchell, *poet and playwright*

William Blake Says:
Every Thing That Lives is Holy

Long live the Child
Long live the Mother and Father
Long live the People

Long live this wounded Planet
Long live the good milk of the Air
Long live the spawning Rivers and the
                    mothering Oceans
Long live the juice of the Grass
and all the determined greenery of the Globe

Long live the Elephants and the Sea Horses,
the Humming-Birds and the Gorillas,
the Dogs and Cats and Field-Mice –
all the surviving Animals
our innocent Sisters and Brothers

Long live the Earth, deeper than all our thinking

we have done enough killing

Long live the Man
Long live the Woman
Who use both courage and compassion
Long live their Children

Adrian Mitchell (1932–)

Dr Arthur Mitchell, *GP and beekeeper in the Mourne Mountains*

~

I wonder what it's like to be as good, as good, as gold,
For that's how good I ought to be, I'm always being told.
I'd like to be like gold, just once, just so that I could see.
But I wonder what would gold be like, if gold were as good as me!

Anon.

'This was taught to me by my mother, a Montessori teacher. It was only when I was much older that I realized its significance.'

Lady Morse, *author and London tourist guide*

~

Leave me, O Love, which reachest but to dust;
And thou, my mind, aspire to higher things;
Grow rich in that which never taketh rust;
Whatever fades, but fading pleasure brings.
Draw in thy beams, and humble all thy might
To that sweet yoke, where lasting freedoms be;
Which breaks the clouds, and opens forth the light
That doth both shine and give us sight to see.
O take fast hold; let that light be thy guide
In this small course which birth draws out to death,
And think how evil becometh him to slide,
Who seeketh heaven, and comes of heavenly breath.
    Then farewell, world; thy uttermost I see;
    Eternal Love, maintain thy life in me.

Sir Philip Sidney (1554–86)

Sir Jeremy Morse, *banker and Chancellor of Bristol University*

He that knows not and knows not that he knows not,
    Shun him, for he is a fool.
He that knows not and knows that he knows not,
    Teach him, for he will learn.
He that knows and knows not that he knows,
    Wake him, for he is asleep.
He that knows and knows that he knows,
    Follow him, for his is wise.

Persian proverb (sometimes said to be Indian)

'Taught to me by my school master when I was nine and which I have never forgotten.'

Also chosen by **Sir Geoffrey Dear**, *police officer.*

We sail a changeful sea through halcyon days and storm,
And when the ship laboureth, our steadfast purpose
Trembles like the compass in a binnacle.
Our stability is but balance, and conduct lies
In masterful administration of the unforeseen.

Robert Bridges (1844–1930), from *The Testament of Beauty*, Book 1

Sir John Mortimer, *barrister, playwright and author*

They say the seeds of what we will do are in all of us, but it always seemed to me that in those who make jokes in life the seeds are covered with better soil and with a higher grade of manure.

Ernest Hemingway (1899–1961), from *A Moveable Feast*

Dr Basil Mustafa, *Nelson Mandela Fellow, Oxford Centre for Islamic Studies*

The famous Muslim jurist Al-Shaafi'* was asked: 'What is the proof for the existence of God?'

He replied: 'The mulberry tree. Its colour, smell, taste and everything about it seem one and the same to you. But a caterpillar eats it and it comes out as fine silken thread. A bee feeds on it and it comes out as honey. A sheep eats it and it comes out as dung. Gazelles chew on it and it congeals, producing the fragrance of musk.

Who made all these different things come from the same type of tree?'

Hassan Ayoud, from *Islamic Theology Made Simple*

¶ *Al Shaafi' (cAH 150–204 [820AD])

The Rt Hon. Sir Patrick Nairne, *former Master of St Catherine's College, Oxford*

◠

Example is not the main thing in influencing others – it is the only thing.

Albert Schweitzer (1875–1965)

I am against the legal minimum wallah every time.

Field Marshal Lord Slim (1891–1970)

'I came across these two quotations when I was young and I have valued them since, particularly while doing my best as a leader, as an infantry officer in the war, as a civil servant and then as master of a college.

I also enjoy the Revd Sydney Smith's advice to his friend Lady Georgiana Morpeth.'

Foston, Feb. 16th, 1820

Dear Lady Georgiana,

… Nobody has suffered more from low spirits than I have done – so I feel for you. 1st Live as well as you dare. 2nd Go into the shower-bath with a small quantity of water at a temperature low enough to give you a slight sensation of cold, 75° or 80°. 3rd Amusing books. 4th Short views of human life – not further than dinner or tea. 5th Be as busy as you can. 6th See as much as you can of those friends who respect and like you. 7th And of those acquaintances who amuse you. 8th Make no secret of low spirits to your friends, but talk of them freely – they are always worse for dignified conceal-ment. 9th Attend to the effects tea and coffee produce upon you. 10th Compare your lot with that of other people. 11th Don't expect too much from human life – a sorry business at the best. 12th Avoid poetry, dramatic representations (except comedy), music, serious novels, melancholy sentimental people, and everything likely to excite feeling or emotion not ending in active benevolence. 13th *Do good,* and endeavour to please everybody of every degree. 14th Be as much as you can in the open air without fatigue. 15th Make the room where you commonly sit, gay and pleasant. 16th Struggle by little and little against idleness. 17th Don't be too severe upon yourself, or underrate yourself, but do yourself justice. 18th Keep good blazing fires. 19th Be firm and constant in the exercise of rational religion. 20th Believe me, dear Lady Georgiana,

> Very truly yours,
> Sydney Smith

Rabbi Julia Neuberger, *writer and broadcaster, chief executive of The King's Fund*

~

... 'Give me your tired, your poor,
Your huddled masses yearning to breathe free,
The wretched refuse of your teeming shore.
Send these, the homeless, tempest-tost to me,
I lift my lamp beside the golden door!'

Emma Lazarus (1849–87), from *The New Colossus*

' Emma Lazarus was born into a Sephardic Jewish family in New York. The poem appears on the plinth of the Statue of Liberty in New York. The statue was given to the United States of America by the people of France.

Give Us This Day

Today I pray for one thing,
Tomorrow quite another,
I am afraid that I give God
An awful lot of bother.

Josephine Royle

¶ Josephine Royle was an American poet. Her work appears in Edwin Markham's *The Book of American Poetry* (1934) but no further information can be traced.

John Julius Norwich, *author and broadcaster*

There is hardly anything in the world that some man cannot make a little worse and sell a little cheaper, and the people who consider price only are this man's lawful prey.

John Ruskin (1819–1900)

Cardinal Cormac Murphy O'Connor, *Cardinal Archbishop of Westminster*

… Let him so temper all things that the strong may have something to strive for and the weak nothing to dismay them.

St Benedict (*c.* 480–547), from *The Rule of St Benedict*, Chapter 64: Concerning the appointment of the Abbot and the discretion and moderation he should show to the Brethren.

Revd John Oliver, *retired naval chaplain*

O hearken for this is wonder!
Light looked down and beheld Darkness.
'Thither will I go,' said Light.
Peace looked down and beheld War.
'Thither will I go,' said Peace.
Love looked down and beheld Hatred.
'Thither will I go,' said Love.
So came Light, and shone.
So came Peace, and gave rest.
So came Love and brought Life.
And the Word was made Flesh, and dwelt among us.

Laurence Housman (1865–1959), from 'Brother Sun', *Little Plays of St Francis*

The Rt Hon. Lord Owen, *politician and statesman*

Their Love Brings You to My Heart

They who are near to me do not know that you are nearer to me than they are.

They who speak to me do not know that my heart is full with your unspoken words.

They who crowd in my path do not know I am walking alone with you.

They who love me do not know that their love brings you to my heart.

Rabindranath Tagore (1861–1941)

¶ This poem was originally thought of as a song. This is Tagore's own translation.

John Wyn Owen, *Secretary of Health Services Research Trust*

⌒

Time to be slow, time to dream, time to read. One of the biggest luxuries in modern life is unscheduled, uncommitted time. Defend it fiercely and value it.

Ilse Crawford (1959–), from *Sensual Home*

Leisure

What is this life if, full of care,
We have no time to stand and stare?

No time to stand beneath the boughs
And stare as long as sheep or cows.

No time to see, when woods we pass,
Where squirrels hide their nuts in grass.

No time to see, in broad daylight,
Streams full of stars, like skies at night.

No time to turn at Beauty's glance,
And watch her feet, how they can dance.

No time to wait till her mouth can
Enrich that smile her eyes began.

A poor life this if, full of care,
We have not time to stand and stare.

W. H. Davies (1870–1940)

Sir Christopher Paine, *oncologist and radiologist, retired Chairman of the Royal Society of Medicine*

LEPIDUS: Noble friends
That which combined us was most great, and let not
A leaner action rend us. What's amiss,
May it be gently heard; when we debate
Our trivial difference loud, we do commit
Murder in healing wounds: then, noble partners,
(The rather, for I earnestly beseech,)
Touch you the sourest points with sweetest terms,
Nor curstness grow to the matter.

ANTONY: 'Tis spoken well.
Were we before our armies and to fight,
I should do thus.

William Shakespeare (1564–1616), from *Antony and Cleopatra*, Act II, Scene ii

Those who carry on great public schemes must be proof against the most fatiguing delays, the most mortifying disappointments, the most shocking insults and, what is worst of all, the presumptuous judgement of the ignorant.

Edmund Burke (1729–97)

❡ Edmund Burke was born in Dublin of mixed Protestant and Roman Catholic parents, and came to London in 1750. His influence as diplomat, political thinker, parliamentarian and orator spanned 30 years of turmoil and development in world politics.

The Rt Hon. Sir Michael Palliser, *retired head of the Diplomatic Service and Foreign and Commonwealth Office*

～

It is the nature and the advantage of strong people that they can bring out the crucial questions and form a clear opinion about them. The weak always have to decide between alternatives which are not their own.

Dietrich Bonhoeffer (1906–45)

'I was impressed by this quotation which I came across some time ago. Pastor Bonhoeffer was murdered on 9 April 1945. I spent that day in my tank advancing along the north German plain, shortly before the German capitulation – it was my 23rd birthday.'

¶ Bonhoeffer was hanged in Flossenberg concentration camp on 9 April 1945. A week later the camp was liberated by the Allies.

When a man is tired of London, he is tired of life; for there is in London all that life can afford.

Dr. Samuel Johnson (1709–84), quoted in Boswell's *Life of Samuel Johnson*, 20 September 1777

'Having lived for over 50 years in London (when not 'on Her Majesty's Service' in foreign parts), I have an abiding affection for our capital city, and heartily endorse the Doctor's judgement.'

Geoffrey Palmer, *actor*

I would never stop fishing because I do not want to lose what goes with fishing, this last connection to everything. It is an extension of your whole organism into the environment that has created us. It is a form of meditation, of communion with levels of self that are deeper than the ordinary self. If I were deprived of this it would be as if I had had some vital part of me amputated.

Jung used to say that most of his patients would be cured if only they could reimmerse themselves in the primitive man or woman for five minutes. Fishing and hunting do this, they reimmerse you in levels of interconnectedness within yourself. They become important to your well-being. If ever they abolish fishing I would have to leave the country. I'd have to go and live in a land where I can still keep hold of the world.

Taken from an interview with Ted Hughes in *Wild Steelhead and Salmon Magazine*

Pike

Pike, three inches long, perfect
Pike in all parts, green tigering the gold.
Killers from the egg: the malevolent aged grin.
They dance on the surface among the flies.

Or move stunned by their own grandeur,
Over a bed of emerald, silhouette
Of submarine delicacy and horror,
A hundred feet long in their world.

[…]

A pond I fished, fifty yards across,
Whose lilies and muscular tench
Had outlasted every visible stone
Of the monastery that planted them –

Stilled legendary depth:
It was as deep as England. It held
Pike too immense to stir, so immense and old
That past nightfall I dared not cast

But silently cast and fished
With the hair frozen on my head
For what might move, for what eye might move.
The still splashes on the dark pond,

Owls hushing the floating woods
Frail on my ear against the dream
Darkness beneath night's darkness had freed,
That rose slowly towards me, watching.

Ted Hughes (1930–98), Poet Laureate 1984–98

Brian Patten, *poet*

⌒

Two Men from the Same Town

I was standing at a crossroads
When a man came to me and said,
'Can you tell me what it's like
In that town up ahead?'
I asked him what it had been like
In the town through which he'd passed.
He said it had been a dreadful place.
I said, 'You'll find the next place like the last.'
Soon as he was gone, another man came by;
He too asked if the place ahead
Was a good place in which to stay.
I asked *him* what it had been like
In the town through which he'd passed.
He said it had been quite wonderful.
I said, 'You'll find the next place like the last.'

Brian Patten (1946–) based on a traditional story

Elizabeth Peer, *artist*

~

Set me as a seal upon your heart,
As a seal upon your arm;
For love is strong as death, passion fierce as the grave.
Its flashes are flashes of fire, a raging flame.
Many waters cannot quench love,
Neither can floods drown it.
If one offered for love all the wealth of one's house,
It would be utterly scorned.

Song of Solomon Ch. 8 vv. 6–7 (NRSV)

Jamie Pegge, *pupil, Wrington Church of England Primary School*

~

The Creation

The first of the living is dead
The first of the night is now day,
The first in the making is made,
All cattle lie in the hay,
Bright is the new light in the empty sky.

Jamie Pegge aged 10, written for the 'Threshold Prize' charity

Major General Brian Pennicott, *gentleman usher and retired soldier*

~

If something is worrying or annoying you, write a letter about it but DON'T necessarily post it.

'This advice was given to me by my father.'

Mary Perks, *managing director of department store*

~

… When, in planning a tale or living a life one encounters a locked door, it is as well not at once to force the lock but to turn aside from it, to do something else, to go to sleep perhaps, and to wait; for in the end, if we do not rattle and bang, doors often open themselves that have anything for us on the other side. And if there is nothing on their other side that we are capable of receiving naturally and tranquilly, it is as well that they should remain shut. A great part of the world's energy has been spent in breaking into prison. In the end, all violence proves itself to have been unintelligent.

Charles Morgan (1894–1958), Introduction to *The River Line*

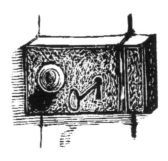

The Very Revd John F. Petty, *Dean Emeritus of Coventry Cathedral*

⌒

The Kingdom of God is the sum of right relationships.

Attributed to William Temple (1881–1944)

'In the Lord's Prayer we pray, "Thy Kingdom come". It is what we need and seek. Relationships may be with God, the world, the family, but begin with oneself.

I discovered empirically at Coventry Cathedral that at all the different levels there are four steps: penitence; forgiveness; reconciliation; healing/peace.

Get these right and the Kingdom is glimpsed. The key to it all is love and God is love.'

Because of His visitation, we may no longer desire God as if He were lacking: our redemption is no longer a question of pursuit but a surrender to Him who is always and everywhere present. Therefore at every moment we pray that following Him we may depart from our anxiety to His peace.

W. H. Auden (1907–73), from *For the Time Being*

Tom Pevsner, *retired film producer*

In India, think Indian.

'In 1982, on a plane between Bombay and Delhi, I picked up a *Times of India* newspaper, and came across this headline from an article, the subject of which I have long forgotten.

At the time I was in negotiation with various Indian authorities over permits and facilities needed to film location sequences in Udaipur for the James Bond film *Octopussy*. The negotiations were not progressing well, and I was increasingly frustrated by what I perceived as Indian intransigence about and lack of understanding for our requirements.

The headline brought me up short, and by the time I got to Delhi, I had understood that in order to reach agreement with people of a different but equally valid culture I had to see the situation from their point of view. The headline remained on the wall as a permanent reminder.'

Tim Pigott-Smith, *actor and director*

No one passes through life scatheless. The world has many sour noises, the body is an open target for many invisible enemies, all hurtful, some venomous, like the accursed virus which can bite deeply into flesh and mind. It is full of disappointments, and too many of us have to suffer the loss of a beloved child, a wound that aches bitterly till our time here ends. Yet, even so, each one of us, one time or another, can ride a white horse, can have rings on our fingers and bells on our toes, and, if we keep our senses open to the scents, sounds and sights all around us, we shall have music wherever we go.

Sean O'Casey (1884–1964), from 'The Bald Primaqueera', *Blasts and Benedictions*

'I feel rather about wisdom, as I do about rules – there is only one rule, and that is – There are *no* rules. Wisdom, seems to me, to be realizing what could have helped you just after the ship has hit the rocks. I think this notion – written by the great Irish playwright, Sean O'Casey, two weeks before his death – is of more practical use.'

Professor Sir Ghillean Prance, *retired director of Kew Gardens*

⤳

Ua Mau ke ea o ka aina I ka pono.
[The life of the land is perpetuated in righteousness.]

Motto of native Hawaii

How long will the land mourn
and the grass of every field wither?
For the wickedness of those who live in it,
The animals and the birds are swept away,
And because the people said 'He is blind to our ways.'

Jeremiah 12: 4 (NRSV)

'On a recent sabbatical to Hawaii, I learned a lot about its people and their attitude to the land. This is in marked contrast to the way in which we Westerners have destroyed our land. I was struck by their motto and reminded of Jeremiah's lament and the need for us to take better care of the soil and the land which are particularly precious God-given resources.'

Rosalind Preston, *co-chair, Interfaith Network UK*

⤳

You are the bows from which your children as living arrows are sent forth.
    The Archer sees the mark upon the path of the infinite, and He bends you with His might, that His arrows may go swift and far.
    Let your bending in the Archer's hand be for gladness.
    For even as He loves the arrow that flies, so He loves also the bow that is stable.

Kahlil Gibran (1883–1931), from *The Prophet*

Ranchor Prime, *author and teacher of Hinduism*

⌒

The Eternal Soul

There never was a time when I, you, and all these warriors here did not exist, and there never will be a time when any of us shall cease to be.

As the self travels in this body from childhood to youth to old age, so the self moves into another body at death. The wise are not confused by this change.

Happiness and distress appear and disappear like winter and summer. They arise from the perceptions of the senses and you must learn to tolerate them without being disturbed.

The soul exists forever in the present, having no birth or death. The soul is the oldest, without beginning or end, and is not killed when the body is killed.

As a person exchanges old clothes for new, so the soul abandons old bodies to enter new ones.

The soul cannot be cut by weapons, nor burned by fire, nor moistened by water, nor withered by wind.

This soul cannot be pierced, burned, wet or dried. For the soul is everlasting, all-pervading, unchangeable and immovable, staying eternally the same.

Bhagavad Gita, 11, 12–24

Words spoken by Krishna (God in human form) to his friend Arjuna when, at the moment of battle in a great war, Arjuna is overcome with fear and distress and turns to Krishna for help.

The Hon. Sir Peter Ramsbotham, *retired diplomat and former Chairman of the Ryder-Cheshire Foundation*

W e will find that it is in going out to help someone whose need is greater than ours that we solve our own problems and become fulfilled as a person; more fully the unique masterpiece that God wills us ultimately to be.

Leonard Cheshire (1917–92), from *The Hidden World*

'I met Leonard Cheshire 30 years ago when my daughter broke her neck and back. He was a great inspiration in my life, as indeed has been this paragraph at the close of his book.'

¶ In August 1945 Leonard Cheshire, an RAF bomber pilot, was an observer at the dropping of the atom bomb on Hiroshima. Subsequently, he founded the Cheshire Home Charity, which cares for physically and mentally disabled people around the world. Becoming himself a victim of motor neurone disease, he said to a friend 'Now I really know how it feels to be in a wheelchair.'

Professor Martin J. Rees, *Royal Society Professor of Astronomy*

~~

'One thing astronomy teaches us is that we are not only the outcome of billions of years of evolution, but that the Earth has a future that could be equally prolonged. We should not see ourselves as the culmination of evolution. What happens now on Earth not only affects our own lives and those of our children, but could foreclose a marvellous future as prolonged as our past. This perspective should give us all a stronger motive to cherish the Earth, this tiny pale blue dot in the cosmos which is our home.

I enjoy the quotation from Thomas Wright but it manifests a degree of detachment from the world's problems that I can't share!'

In this great Celestial Creation, even the total Dissolution of a System of Worlds may be no more to the great Author of Nature than the most common Accident of Life with us, and in all Probability such final Dooms Days may be as frequent there as even Birth Days with us upon this Earth.

This idea has something so cheerful in it, that I can never look upon the Stars without wondering why the whole World does not become Astronomers … and reconcile them to all those little Difficulties incident to human Nature, without the least Anxiety.

Thomas Wright of Durham (1711–86), from *An Original Theory of New Hypothesis of the Universe* (1750)

❡ Thomas Wright, philosopher and mathematician, anticipated the modern physico-philosophical theory of the material universe. He was offered, but declined, the Chair of Mathematics at the Imperial Academy of St Petersburg.

Lord Vinson suggested this observation by Leonardo da Vinci:

Though human genius in its various inventions with various instruments may answer the same end, it will never find an invention more beautiful or more simple or more direct than nature, because in her inventions nothing is lacking and nothing [is] superfluous.

Leonardo da Vinci (1452–1519)

Dr Marjorie Reeves, *historian, university teacher and retired Vice-Principal of St Anne's College, Oxford*

⌒

Fergal Keane, writing on the events of September 11th 2001:

There was phone call after phone call from those trapped in doomed airliners or in the crumbling World Trade Center. Again and again they told those they were leaving behind: 'I love you.' Those three words are the most important in our language.

Fergal Keane (1961–), the *Independent*, 17 September 2001

A person's faith is his [*sic*] supreme principle of valuation. It is only by our faith that we can decide what is most worth having in life ... The life that is without a persistent and controlling principle of order in its choices is a life without order and without sanity.

John Macmurray* (1891–1976), from *Freedom in the Modern World*

¶ * Grote Professor of Philosophy and Logic, University of London, and Professor of Moral Philosophy, University of Edinburgh.

Sir William Reid, *retired ombudsman*

⌒

Every book is, in an intimate sense, a circular letter to the friends of him who writes it. They alone take his meaning; they find private messages, assurances of love, and expressions of gratitude dropped for them in every corner.

Robert Louis Stevenson (1850–94), from the dedicatory letter to *Travels with a Donkey in the Cevennes*

I have never thought it easy to be just, and find it daily even harder than I thought.

Robert Louis Stevenson (1850–94), from *Travels with a Donkey in the Cevennes*

Sir Cliff Richard, *singer*

⌒

O Lord my God! When I in awesome wonder
Consider all the works Thy hand hath made;
I see the stars, I hear the mighty thunder,
Thy pow'r throughout the universe displayed:

> Then sings my soul, my Saviour God, to Thee,
> How great Thou art! How great Thou art!
> Then sings my soul, my Saviour God, to Thee,
> How great Thou art! How great Thou art!

When through the woods and forest glades I wander
And hear the birds sing sweetly in the trees;
When I look down from lofty mountain grandeur,
And hear the brook, and feel the gentle breeze:

And when I think that God, His Son not sparing,
Sent Him to die – I scarce can take it in:
That on the Cross, my burden gladly bearing,
He bled and died to take away my sin:

When Christ shall come with shout of acclamation
And take me home – what joy shall fill my heart!
Then shall I bow in humble adoration,
And there proclaim, my God how great Thou art!

Stuart K. Hine (1899–1989)

❡ Hine was working in the Carpathian Mountains when he found the Russian translation of a hymn, 'O Store Gud' by the Swedish pastor, Carl Boberg (1856–1940), which inspired this popular hymn. Boberg, the son of a carpenter, was dramatically converted at the age of nineteen. He became a pastor and later a representative in the Swedish upper parliament. He wrote his original nine-stanza poem in 1886, after he had witnessed an awesome storm, and it was later set to a Swedish folk melody. Boberg's hymn also inspired Eluned Harrison to write her own version, which appears in the Welsh Hymn Book. Patrick Hort made a translation of the original for reference in this book. His rendering of verse 8 is:

When torn by guilt I kneel in humble worship
At mercy's throne and pray for grace and peace,
When Jesus guides my frail and wavering footsteps
And rescues me from all my sins and strife;

John Romer, *Egyptologist*

⌒

What makes a steel axe superior to a stone axe is not that the first one is better made than the second. They are equally well made, but steel is quite different from stone. We may be able to show that the same logical process operates in myth as in science, and that man has always been thinking equally well; the improvement lies not in any alleged progress of man's mind but in the discovery of new areas to which it may apply its unchanging powers.

Claude Lévi-Strauss* (1908–), from *Structural Anthropology*

'This quotation is not merely technical. It always seemed to me that to assume that the distant past was "primitive" gives prejudice a pedigree.'

¶ *Professor of Anthropology at Sao Paolo and other universties.

Christine van Ruymbeke, *lecturer in Persian*

⌒

If you fall into a deep pit the fates are not obliged to get you out.

Medieval Persian saying

Dr Jonathan Sacks, *Chief Rabbi of the United Hebrew Congregations of the Commonwealth*

'Many centuries ago Judaism's ancient sages made two wonderful statements about the nature of courage. The first belongs to a Rabbi known as Ben [son of] Zoma. Quoting the Book of Proverbs – "He who is slow to anger is better than the mighty, and he who rules over the spirits is greater than one who conquers a city"– he asked, "Who is a hero?" His answer? Not "one who prevails over an enemy" but "one who masters his own evil impulse". True strength is not the ability to restrain others but to restrain oneself. That is why peace is always a greater and more strenuous challenge than war.

That was a fine insight, but greater still was the lovely saying of the sages who came after him. They said: "Who is a hero? One who turns an enemy into a friend."

Nothing is harder, but nothing more necessary if we are to keep faith with the future and preserve for our children the lineaments of hope.'

Alice Basil Sahhar, *founder and Director of Jeel Al-Amal Home for Children, East Jerusalem*

Children all over the world are the same – Angels walking on earth. For in what language does a baby cry?

Alice Basil Sahhar

¶ Alice Basil Sahhar is a Palestinian Christian. She writes: 'Jeel Al-Amal means "Generation of Hope" because we raise the children to be hopeful despite their difficult situation. We have girls as well as boys and take in babies when they have nowhere to go. They all need our love.'

The Rt Revd and Rt Hon. Mark Santer, *Bishop Emeritus of Birmingham*

There is no moment at which God does not present himself under the guise of some suffering, some consolation or some duty. All that occurs within us, around us and by our means covers and hides his divine action. His action is there, most really and certainly present, but in an invisible manner, so we are always being taken by surprise and only recognize his operation after it has passed. Could we pierce the veil and were we vigilant, God would reveal himself continuously to us. At every occurrence we should say: *Dominus est.* It is the Lord; and in all circumstances we should find a gift from God.

If we lived uninterruptedly by the life of faith we should be in continual contact with God, we should speak with him face to face. As the air is the medium for transmitting our thoughts and words to others, so all our deeds or sufferings would transmit to us the thoughts and words of God. All would be holy and excellent. This union with God will be established in heaven by glory; faith will establish it on earth and the only difference is in our mode of reception.

Jean-Pierre de Caussade (1675–1751)

¶ It is sometimes said that the teaching of Caussade is crystallized in the phrase 'the sacrament of the present moment'.

Zia Sardar, *writer and critic*

෴

Consider the flight of time:
Verily man is bound to lose himself
Save those who believe and do good works,
And counsel upon one another the keeping of truth.
And counsel upon one another the patience in adversity.

'This is the complete Chapter 103 of the Qur'an entitled "The Declining Day". They are the first verses of the Qur'an I learned by heart. They have brought me solace and hope, particularly when things were not going well, and I often find myself unconsciously reciting them. Most of my writing, and much of my thought, is shaped by their advice.'

Jehngir Sarosh, *President of World Conference of Religions for Peace (Europe)*

෴

Light up the candle
Look into the light
And know you are loved
Be well – get well
For the sake of love
And be, for you are.

A Zoroastrian bidding

The Rt Hon. Lord Justice Schiemann, *Lord Justice of Appeal*

❧

Blessed is the man whose strength is in You:
In whose heart are the highways to Zion;

Who going through the valley of dryness
Finds there is a spring from which to drink:
Till the autumn rain shall clothe it with blessings.

Psalm 84, verses 5 and 6 (ASB)

'It has seemed to me that those who approach some horror in that spirit, and who can turn a negative into a positive, can bear much fruit.'

Paul Scofield, *actor*

❧

Every moment some form grows perfect in hand or face; some tone on the hills or the sea is choicer than the rest; some mood of passion or insight or intellectual excitement is irresistibly real and attractive for us – for that moment only. Not the fruit of experience, but experience itself, is the end. A counted number of pulses only is given to us of a variegated, dramatic life. How may we see in them all that is to be seen by the finest senses? … To burn always with this hard, gemlike flame, to maintain this ecstasy, is success in life … While all melts under our feet, we may well catch at any exquisite passion, or any contribution to knowledge that seems by a lifted horizon to set the spirit free for a moment, or any stirring of the senses, strange dyes, strange colours, and curious odours, or work of the artist's hands.

Walter Pater (1839–94), from *Studies in the History of the Renaissance*

❡ This passage comes at the end of the essay on Leonardo da Vinci and the evocation of the *Mona Lisa*.

Richard Scott, *retired Chairman of the Association of Grain Millers*

～

Ode on Solitude

Happy the man, whose wish and care
　　A few paternal acres bound,
Content to breathe his native air,
　　In his own ground.

Whose herds with milk, whose fields with bread,
　　Whose flocks supply him with attire,
Whose trees in summer yield him shade,
　　In winter fire.

Blest! Who can unconcern'dly find
　　Hours, days, and years slide soft away,
In health of body, peace of mind,
　　Quiet by day.

Sound sleep by night: study and ease,
　　Together mixed; sweet recreation:
And innocence, which most does please,
　　With meditation.

Thus let me live, unseen, unknown;
　　Thus unlamented let me die;
Steal from the world, and not a stone
　　Tell where I lie.

Alexander Pope (1688–1744)

'Pope modelled his poem on Horace's second epode. It was first composed when he was eleven or twelve years old and was included in a letter to Richard Cromwell on 17 July 1709. Cromwell's reply is not recorded.'

Professor Roger Scruton, *philosopher and broadcaster*

↢

1. To seek lasting truth in fashionable literature is to hope for a diamond in the mouth of a fish.
2. The charlatan is the one who declares sovereignty over truth.

'Two of the laws of academic life that I have formulated, as a result of 30 years' experience of universities.'

Michael Selby, *retired prison governor*

↢

A faith is something you die for; a doctrine is something you kill for; there is all the difference in the world.

Tony Benn (1925–)

The Christian religion is strong on gratitude. It teaches that gratitude is not just a debt owed to the past but rather a capacity of sensible people to recognize themselves as being blessed. It is the most secure motive of moral standards. The cure for most of the things we deplore lies not so much in a sterner sense of duty but in greater awareness of our blessings.

Perhaps it is the wisdom of knowing that we are blessed that will create harmony from conflict, unite the wise and foolish and remind us that to whom much is given, of them shall much be required.

Conclusion of a sermon by Lord Runcie in the chapel of Queens' College,
Cambridge, celebrating its 550th anniversary

Fatima Sharipova, *guide in Bukhara and Samarkand, Uzbekistan*

～

D̲ilba yor,
Dastba kor.

[God in your heart and labour in your hands.]

Nakshbandi (1318–83), Sufi mystic

❡ Nakshbandi reformed the Sufi movement which he found to be over-pious and too dependent on society for physical support. Trained as a metal-worker, he became a scholar and disciplined himself to hard labour in road-building and animal care. His shrine lies close to Bukhara. Pilgrims move quietly round the saint's black tomb. Others prepare feasts with a great deal of noise in the large, semi-open, communal kitchens.

Judy Shercliffe, *volunteer cathedral guide and teacher*

～

Go forth into the world in peace;
be of good courage;
hold fast that which is good;
render to no man evil for evil;
strengthen the faint-hearted;
support the weak; help the afflicted;
honour all men; love and serve the Lord;
rejoicing in the power of the Holy Spirit;
and the blessing of God Almighty,
the Father, the Son and the Holy Ghost be upon you
and remain with you for ever.

Confirmation Blessing from the 1928 Prayer Book

'I think often of this prayer, also of a saying useful to service wives:'

Grow where you are planted.

Deborah Silvey, *teacher, Los Angeles*

And Yet the Books

And yet the books will be there on the shelves, separate beings,
That appeared once, still wet
As shining chestnuts under a tree in autumn,
And, touched, coddled, began to live
In spite of fires on the horizon, castles blown up,
Tribes on the march, planets in motion.
'We are,' they said, even as their pages
Were being torn out, or a buzzing flame
Licked away their letters. So much more durable
Than we are, whose frail warmth
Cools down with memory, disperses, perishes.
I imagine the earth when I am no more:
Nothing happens, no loss, it's still a strange pageant,
Women's dresses, dewy lilacs, a song in the valley.
Yet the books will be there on the shelves, well born,
Derived from people, but also from radiance, heights.

Czeslaw Milosz (1911–), trans. Robert Hass.

'Born in Lithuania, the son of a civil engineer, Milosz (a former US Poet Laureate) spent most of the Second World War in Warsaw, working for the underground press. He won the Nobel Prize for Literature in 1980.'

Richard Skinner, *writer and therapist*

True wisdom lies in doing what you are doing.

Meister Eckhartd (?1260–?1327)

The soul is nearer to God than it is to the body, which makes us human. It is more intimate with Him than a drop of water put into a vat of wine, for that would still be water and wine; but here one is changed into the other so that no creature could ever again detect a difference between them.

❡ Johannes Eckhartd (known as Meister Eckhartd) is widely regarded as the founder of German Mysticism. A Dominican, he taught in Paris and preached in Germany, but was later accused of heresy and obliged to recant some of his opinions. He died before the hearings were completed.

The Very Revd Dr Stephen S. Smalley,
Dean Emeritus of Chester

~

Beloved, let us love one another, because love is from God; everyone who loves is born of God and knows God. Whoever does not love does not know God, for God is love. God's love was revealed among us in this way: God sent his only Son into the world so that we might live through him. In this is love, not that we loved God but that he loved us and sent his Son to be the atoning sacrifice for our sins. Beloved, since God loved us so much, we also ought to love one another. No one has ever seen God; if we love one another, God lives in us, and his love is perfected in us.

I John 4: 7–12 (NRSV)

'I have chosen this text because of my interest and research into John in the New Testament, and also because I believe that love changes everything.'

❡ Stephen Smalley translates the last phrase as 'his love has been brought to completion in us' in his *Letters of John* (Word Books, 1984).

Tim Smit, *Chief Executive Officer of The Eden Project*

~

The graveyards of the world are full of implacable people.

General Charles de Gaulle (1890–1970) from Ernest Mignon, *Les Mots du Général.*

Bill Smith, *National Hunt Jockey to*
the late Queen Elizabeth The Queen Mother

~

If you cannot be part of the solution don't become part of the problem.

The Revd Howard Smith, *hospital chaplain*

⌒

A flower on earth
lent not given,
to bud on earth
and bloom in heaven.

Anon.

'This simple verse has helped bereaved parents and is often used on grave-stones.'

¶ It is sometimes wrongly said that Shelley wrote this when his favourite son, William, died aged three in Rome. The Shelley Society in Rome identi-fied William's grave which lies in the cemetery for foreigners in Testaccio, just outside the centre of Rome. The simple, flat stone bears only the names of William and his parents.

Lady Southey, *philanthropist, Vice-President of the Australian National Stroke Association and President of the Meyer Foundation and Philanthropy, Australia*

⌒

Do it. Do it.

'As a child, hanging in my sister's bedroom was a plaque which said "When in doubt what to do, don't do it." As our lives have turned out we have inclined to the group that says "Do it. Do it." '

Dame Muriel Spark, *author*

I said to the man who stood at the gate of the year, 'Give me light that I may tread safely into the unknown.' And he replied, 'Go out into the darkness and put your hand into the hand of God. That shall be to you better than light and safer than a known way.'

Minnie Louise Haskins (1875–1957). Quoted in the Christmas message of George VI, broadcast 1939.

Also chosen by **Sir Geoffrey Dear**, *Police Officer and former Inspector of Constabulary.*

Friede Springer, *newspaper proprietor* (Der Spiegel)

Heute ist der Tag, der mir gestern so viele Sorgen bereitet hat.

[Today is the day which, yesterday, caused me so much concern.]

Ann Steadman, *teacher*

〜

 W hat will survive of us is love.

Philip Larkin (1922–85), last line from 'An Arundel Tomb'

'This quotation was given to me by the writer Terence de Vere White.'

 K now this, my beloved brethren.
Let every man be quick to hear, slow to
speak, slow to anger, for the anger of
man does not work the righteousness of God.

James 1: 19-20 (RSV)

Tina Sykes, *retired teacher*

〜

 N ever assume anything.

David Tall, *retired submariner and football executive*

〜

 R esurgam

[I shall rise again.]

'This word was written on a wooden sign posted above the door of St Andrew's Church, Plymouth (destroyed with much of the city during its worst air raid in the Second World War). It inspired the people to endure the raids and later to rebuild the city and its mother church. At least three-quarters of the city and docks had been destroyed.'

Dame Kiri Te Kanawa, *singer*

✑

He Wishes for the Cloths of Heaven

Had I the heavens' embroidered cloths,
Enwrought with golden and silver light,
The blue and the dim and the dark cloths
Of night and light and the half-light,
I would spread the cloths under your feet:
But I, being poor, have only my dreams;
I have spread my dreams under your feet;
Tread softly because you tread on my dreams.

W. B. Yeats (1865–1939)

*Also chosen by **Dr Tom Kennedy**, GP.*

The Rt Hon. Baroness Thatcher, *former prime minister*

✑

That which thy fathers bequeathed thee
Earn it anew if thou wouldst possess it.

Johann Wolfgang von Goethe (1749–1832), from *Faust*, Act 1, Scene i

❡ This quotation was given to Lady Thatcher by her father, and she has likewise passed it on to many organizations and friends.

The Rt Revd and Rt Hon. James Thompson,
former Bishop of Bath and Wells

⌐

The most beautiful and deepest experience a man can have is the sense of the mysterious. It is the underlying principle of religion as well of all serious endeavour in art and science. He who never had this experience seems to me, if not dead, then at least blind. To sense that behind anything that can be experienced there is a something that our minds cannot grasp, whose beauty and sublimity reaches us only indirectly: *this* is religiousness.

Albert Einstein (1879–1955), 'Mein Glaubensbekenntnis' [My Credo], recorded in
1932 for the League of Human Rights, trans. Barbara Harshav

'Einstein is also reputed to have said: "God is subtle but he is not malicious."'

❡ The first extract is quoted in Jim Thompson, *Why God? Thinking through Faith*. The original can be found in an article in *Forum and Century*, (1930).

Colin Thubron, *writer and traveller*

⌐

The truth is cruel but it can be loved, and it makes free those who have loved it.

George Santayana (1863–1952), from *Realms of Being*

❡ George Santayana was a Hispanic American philosopher, poet and critic. Born in Madrid, he lived for many years in Boston.

Sue Townsend, *author*

In Germany, the Nazis came for the Communists and I didn't speak up because I was not a Communist. Then they came for the Jews and I didn't speak up because I was not a Jew. Then they came for the trade unionists and I didn't speak up because I was not a trade unionist. Then they came for the Catholics and I was a Protestant so I didn't speak up. Then they came for me … By that time there was no one to speak up for anyone.

Pastor Martin Niemöller (1892–1984), attributed in *Congressional Record,*
14 October 1968

¶ Niemöller was a U-Boat commander in the First World War. Ordained in 1934, he was later dismissed from his post by the Nazi government and incarcerated in a concentration camp from 1937 until the liberation. He survived to become a bishop in the Evangelical Church, President of the World Council of Churches and a leader for world peace.

Marcus Trescothic, *cricketer: opening batsman for Somerset and England*

'Ambitious people dream about what they want to achieve. Reality is putting effort into achieving that dream.'

F. S. Trueman, *cricket commentator and former cricketer*

❦

Being 70 years old is not bad when you consider the alternative!

Maurice Chevalier (1889–1972)

Lord Tugendhat, *banker*

❦

My rule always was to do the business of the day on the day.

Arthur Wellesley, 1st Duke of Wellington, (1769–1852), when asked to what he attributed his success

Sir Mark Tully, *journalist*

❦

Death's Secret

It is not true
that death begins after life.
When life stops
death also stops.

Gösta Ågren (1936–), trans. David McDuff

The Most Revd Desmond M. Tutu, *Anglican Archbishop Emeritus of Cape Town*

⌒

While we were yet sinners, Christ died for us.

Romans 5: 8 (AV)

'God loves us. Period. We don't have to earn this love: it is given freely for it is grace.'

John Tydeman, *retired head of BBC Radio Drama*

⌒

The truths which the intellect apprehends directly in the world of full and unimpeded light have something less profound, less necessary than those which life communicates to us against our will in an impression which is material because it enters us through the senses, but yet has a spiritual meaning which it is possible for us to extract.

As for the inner book of unknown symbols, if I tried to read them no one could help me with any rules, for to read them is an act of creation in which no one can do our work for us or even collaborate with us. For instinct dictates our duty and the intellect supplies us with pretexts for evading it. But excuses have no place in art and intentions count for nothing: at every moment the artist has to listen to his instinct, and it is this that makes art the most real of all things, the most austere school of life, the true last judgement.

Marcel Proust (1871–1922), from *À la recherche du temps perdu*,
trans. Terence Kilmartin

Most Venerable Pandith M. Vajiragnana, *Sangha Nayaka of Great Britain, head of the London Buddhist Vihara*

〜

As a solid rock is not shaken by the wind, even so the wise are not ruffled by praise or blame.

As a flower that is lovely, beautiful and scent-laden, even so fruitful is the well-spoken word of one who practises it.

The Buddha, Dhammapada, verses 52 and 81

Just as a mother would protect her only child at the risk of her own life, even so, let one cultivate a boundless heart towards all beings.

Let thoughts of infinite love pervade the whole world – above, below and around – without any obstruction, without any hatred, without any enmity.

Whether standing, walking, sitting or lying down, as long as one is awake, this mindfulness should be developed. This, they say, is the Highest Conduct here.

The Buddha, Karaniya Metta Sutta and Khuddaka Nikaya

Lord Vinson, *inventor, industrialist and farmer*

꩜

Intuition is reason in a hurry.

'This is one of twelve aphorisms chosen as engravings on twelve plates brought to her new household by my wife in traditional Danish custom on the occasion of our wedding.

Perhaps one day there will be a scientific explanation, but deep in the psyche of most of us – and women in particular – is the innate ability to come up with an initial judgement which so often proves right.'

Blame not before thou hast examined the truth;
Understand first and then rebuke.

Ecclesiasticus 11: 7, Apocrypha (AV)

Lord, Thou knowest all our desire, and our secret sighing is not hidden from Thee. Into Thy hands I commend my soul and my prayer: give what Thou seest fit, and fit us for what Thou givest. Give us wisdom to abound, or patience to suffer need; and where the Master placed us, there to be content. Let all our work be done well before we come to die; and let us be gathered into Thine arms, as the harvesters gather a shock* in full season. Let our death be happy; and our happiness beyond the power of death. Amen.

Rowland Williams (1817–70), from *Great Souls at Prayer*

*Group of sheaves set up leaning together to dry.

The Revd Pat Stacy Waddy, *retired missionary (aged 95)*

A Valentine

When I was young and foolish
I heard a wise man say,
'Marry me! Marry me! Marry me!'
But lightly I said 'Nay'.

When I was young and lonely
A letter he did pen,
'Would God that you could love me!'
I laughed and said 'Amen'.

A ring upon my finger
It seemed a pretty token.
I thought a promise lightly made
As lightly could be broken.

Now care and time and children
Have bound me to his side;
And he has a loving wife,
Who had a thoughtless bride.

Did he with man's low cunning
Beguile me to be true?
Or was that thoughtless foolish girl
Yet wiser than she knew?

Mary Rae Campbell

Trust in the Lord, and do good; so you will dwell in the land, and enjoy security. Take delight in the Lord, and he will give you the desires of your heart.

Psalm 37, verses 3–4 (RSV)

Warnings

'My mother often warned us against having a highly developed sense of other people's duty. One of my father's warnings was, "Beware of Holy Matrimony, that insane desire to feed and clothe another man's daughter."

My parents met at a jumble sale and were very content with the bargains of that day. When he returned to Australia, she pursued him in a sailing ship (lost with all hands on its next voyage). I have her account of their wedding service, of the gale which blew away the music and Bishop Stanton's wisdom. On honeymoon, they spent one night in a prison colonized by cockroaches. The simple rectory where I was born nestled beside a coal mine that ran out under the Pacific. Nothing daunted them, then or thereafter; as the old prayer book marriage service ends, they "Did Well and were Not Afraid with Any Amazement".'

> Every man at the beginning doth set forth good wine …
> But thou hast kept the best wine until now.

John 2: 10 (AV)

HRH The Prince of Wales

⌒

The new is in the old concealed, the old is in the new revealed.

'The phrase encapsulates the importance and contemporary relevance of tradition to ALL generations.'

Novum Testamentum in Vetere latet, Vetus in Novo patet

St Augustine of Hippo (354–430), from *Questions on the Heptateuch*, Book 2, 73

❡ This saying handed down in this general form may be derived from St Augustine's words, 'The New Testament is concealed in the Old, the Old is revealed in the New', referring to the whole message and tradition of the two Testaments and not solely to the text.

Sir Peter Wallis, *retired diplomat*

⌒

Ah Love! Could thou and I with Fate conspire
To grasp this sorry Scheme of Things entire,
Would not we shatter it to bits – and then
Remould it nearer to the Heart's Desire!

Edward Fitzgerald (1809–83), from *The Rubáiyát of Omar Khayyám*, ed. 1, xxiii

Mary Whiteley, historian, contributed a second verse:

The Moving Finger writes; and, having writ,
Moves on: nor all thy Piety and Wit
Shall lure it back to cancel half a Line,
Nor all thy Tears wash out a Word of it.

Ibid ed. 1, li

Robert Walrond, *sheep farmer*

And Jesus answering said, A certain man went down from Jerusalem to Jericho, and fell among thieves, which stripped him of his raiment, and wounded him, and departed, leaving him half dead.

And by chance there came down a certain priest that way: and when he saw him, he passed by on the other side.

And likewise a Levite, when he was at the place, came and looked on him, and passed by on the other side.

But a certain Samaritan, as he journeyed, came where he was: and when he saw him, he had compassion on him,

And went to him, and bound up his wounds, pouring in oil and wine, and set him on his own beast, and brought him to an inn, and took care of him.

And on the morrow when he departed, he took out two pence, and gave them to the host, and said unto him, Take care of him; and whatsoever thou spendest more, when I come again, I will repay thee.

Which now of these three, thinkest thou, was neighbour unto him that fell among the thieves?

Luke 10: 30–36 (AV)

Harriet Walter, *actress and writer*

Happiness is the end of all our worldly views and proceedings; and no one can judge for another in what will produce it.

Fanny Burney, in a letter to Marianne Waddington, from Kate Chisholm,
Fanny Burney: Her Life

Why will you, my lovely Friend, give consequence to Trifles by thus putting your Peace in their Power? Is not the World full of severe Misfortunes and real Calamities? & will you fret and look pale about such Nonsense as this? Let me see you on Thursday next 24 December if but for an hour, and let me see you chearful [*sic*] I insist. Your looking dismal can only advertise the paltry Pamphlet which I firmly believe no one out of your own Family has seen and which is now only lying like a dead Kitten on the Surface of a dirty Horsepond [sic].

Mrs Thrale's letter to Fanny, ibid.

The Rt Hon. Lord Weatherill, *former Speaker of the House of Commons*

⤿

When geese fly in formation the thrust of their wings gives the whole flock a 70 per cent greater flying range than would be the case if each bird flew alone.

Furthermore, if a goose falls out of formation it is 'honked' back into position – and if a goose is sick or wounded, two geese drop out to help and protect it. Also – from time to time – the lead goose rotates back into formation and another takes its place in the point position.

John Fraser, the Canadian Speaker, recounted this story at the 1988 Commonwealth Speakers' Conference in Westminster

'I find that the implications of this story are tremendous! Sharing a sense of community and a common direction makes it more likely that we will achieve our objectives. We should all seek to help each other in our journey through life, sharing leadership and taking turns at the hard work.'

Jonathan Webb, *English Rugby Union international player and surgeon*

⌒

I will lift up mine eyes unto the hills, from whence cometh my help.
My help *cometh* from the Lord, which made heaven and earth.
He will not suffer thy foot to be moved: he that keepeth thee will not slumber.
Behold, he that keepeth Israel shall neither slumber nor sleep.
The Lord *is* thy keeper: the Lord *is* thy shade upon thy right hand.
The sun shall not smite thee by day, nor the moon by night.
The Lord shall preserve thee from all evil: he shall preserve thy soul.
The Lord shall preserve thy going out and thy coming in from this time forth, and even for evermore.

Psalm 121 (AV)

Pauline Webb, *writer and broadcaster*

⌒

Do all the good you can,
By all the means you can,
In all the ways you can,
In all the places you can,
At all the times you can,
To all the people you can,
As long as ever you can.

John Wesley (1703–91)

Fay Weldon, *writer*

⌐⌐

'Guilt is to the soul as pain is to the body. A signal for you to stop doing whatever it is you're doing. SO STOP!'

'This is a piece of wisdom I would give to the young.'

Timothy West, *actor and director*

⌐⌐

A great object, which I hope will be impressed upon the mind of this Royal Lady, is a rooted horror of *war*. All the atrocious crimes committed in the years of peace are mere trifles compared with the gigantic evils that stalk over the world in a state of war. God is forgotten in war – every principle of Christian charity trampled upon – human labour destroyed, – human industry extinguished – you see the son, and the husband, and the brother, dying miserably in distant lands – you see the waste of human affections, the breaking of human hearts.

I would say to that Royal child, 'Worship God by loving peace. Pity the stupid, frantic folly of human beings who are always ready to deluge the earth with each other's blood … Say upon your deathbed, 'I have made few orphans in my reign – I have made few widows – my object has been peace. This has been the Christianity of my throne; this is the gospel of my sceptre; in this way have I striven to worship my Redeemer and my Judge.'

Revd Sydney Smith (1771–1845), part of a sermon delivered at St Paul's Cathedral on the accession of Queen Victoria to the throne

Dr Terence Wheeler, *oncologist*

Good judgement comes from experience, and a lot of that comes from bad judgement.

Attributed to Will Rogers (1879–1938)

Never miss a chance to shut up.

Constance Whippman, *barrister*

~

Jenny kissed me when we met,
Jumping from the chair she sat in;
Time, you thief, who love to get
Sweets into your list, put that in:
Say I'm weary, say I'm sad,
Say that health and wealth have missed me,
Say I'm growing old but add,
Jenny kissed me.

James Henry Leigh Hunt (1784–1859)

'This was a favourite of Michael Whippman, civil servant and wise adviser.
    Another favourite quotation of Michael's was from Wordsworth's
"King's College Chapel".'

Give all thou canst; high Heaven rejects the lore
Of nicely calculated less or more,

The poem continues–

So deemed the man who fashioned for the sense
These lofty pillars, spread that branching roof …
Where light and shade repose, where music dwells
Lingering – and wandering on as loth to die;
Like thoughts whose very sweetness yieldeth proof
That they were born for immortality.

William Wordsworth (1770–1850), from 'Inside of King's College Chapel,
Cambridge', *Ecclesiastical Sonnets*, Part III, xliii, 'Tax not the Royal Saint'

The Most Revd and Rt Hon. Dr Rowan Williams,
Archbishop of Canterbury

The family has been perceptively described as an *ecclesiola,* a 'little church'. It has also been described as *schola caritatis,* a 'school of love', a phrase often applied to a monastic community. Both descriptions are most appropriate because the community of the family depends for its continued well-being on a whole series of rituals: the common meals, the commemoration of the dead members of the family, the solemnization of marriages and so on, through which each individual has to learn to stop 'doing his own thing', indulging his own ego, and to attend to the common good. For this reason it is most important for any seeker after holiness to carry out the rituals of the community to which he belongs with the utmost care and devotion – even the simplest of them.

Donald Nicholl (1923–97), from Holiness

❡ Donald Nicholl was a historian and theologian, Professor at Keele and Santa Cruz, CA, universities, Rector of Tantur Institute, Jerusalem and author of *Testing of Hearts*, a striking perception of Jerusalem.

The Rt Hon. Lord Williams of Mostyn, *Leader of the House of Lords (previously Attorney-General)*

Arrival

Not conscious
   that you have been seeking
     suddenly
   you come upon it

the village in the Welsh hills
     dust free
   with no road out
but the one you came in by.

   A bird chimes
   from a green tree
the hour that is no hour
   you know. The river dawdles
to hold a mirror for you
where you may see yourself
   as you are, a traveller
     with the moon's halo
   above him, who has arrived
   after long journeying where he
     began, catching this
   one truth by surprise
that there is everything to look forward to.

R. S. Thomas (1913–2000), from *Later Poems*

'I heard this recited, very poignantly, by Neil Kinnock at the memorial service for Lord Cledwyn.'

The Rt Hon. Lord Wilson of Tillyorn, *Master of Peterhouse, Cambridge and former Governor of Hong Kong*

⌒

There was once a man who lost his axe. He suspected that his neighbour's son had stolen it. When he looked at the boy, his way of walking was that of someone who had stolen an axe; the expression on his face was that of someone who had stolen an axe; his manner of speaking was that of someone who had stolen an axe. There was nothing in his actions or behaviour which did not resemble someone who had stolen an axe.

A short while later, the man found his axe when digging in the hills. When he saw his neighbour's son again the next day, he no longer walked like someone who had stolen an axe; the expression on his face was not that of someone who had stolen an axe; and there was nothing in his actions or behaviour which looked like someone who had stolen an axe.

Lieh-tzu (fourth century BC), Taoist philosopher

Revd Andrew Wingfield Digby, *retired captain of Dorset County Cricket Club*

The Gap

Did Jesus live? And did he really say
The burning words that banish mortal fear?
And are they true? Just this is central, here
The Church must stand or fall. It's Christ we weigh.

All else is off the point: the Flood, the Day
Of Eden, or the Virgin Birth – Have done!
The Question is, did God send us the Son
Incarnate crying Love! Love is the way!

Between the probable and proved there yawns
A gap. Afraid to jump, we stand absurd,
Then see behind us sink the ground and, worse,
Our very standpoint crumbling. Desperate dawns
Our only hope: to leap into the word
That opens up the shattered universe.

Sheldon Vanauken (d. 1996), from *A Severe Mercy*

❡ Sheldon Vanauken was Professor of English at Lynchburg College, Virginia, and a personal friend of C. S. Lewis.

Sydney Wooderson, *Olympic runner, mile and half-mile world record-holder, 1937*

❧

Strong son of God, immortal Love,
Whom we, that have not seen thy face,
By faith, and faith alone, embrace,
Believing where we cannot prove.

Alfred, Lord Tennyson (1809–92), from *In Memoriam*

Virginia Wooderson, *English teacher in Tuscany*

❧

I do not know what I may appear to the world, but to myself I seem to have been only a boy playing on the seashore, and diverting myself in now and then finding a smoother pebble or a prettier shell than ordinary, whilst the great ocean of truth lay all undiscovered before me.

Isaac Newton (1642–1727), from D. Brewster, *Memoirs of Newton*, Vol. 2, Chapter 27

Paul Wotton, *captain of Plymouth Argyll football team*

❧

There is no 'I' in team.

Professor Sir Magdi Yacoub, *cardiothoracic surgeon, pioneer in heart and lung transplants*

❧

Creativity – [producing,] ostensibly out of nothing, something of beauty, order or significance.

Peter Medawar (1915–87), (adapted) from *Creativity – Especially in Science*

¶ The original text is 'Creativity is the faculty of mind or spirit that empowers us to bring into existence, ostensibly out of nothing, something of beauty, order or significance.'

Sheila Young, *housewife*

⤿

They were my Geese that laid the Golden Egg, but never cackled.

Sir Winston Churchill (1874–1965)

'This was said by Winston Churchill of the 12,000 people who passed through Bletchley Park, many of whom worked on breaking the Enigma code.'

Philip Ziegler, *author*

⤿

I do not believe in Belief. But this is the age of faith, and there are so many militant creeds that, in self-defence, one has to formulate a creed of one's own … Tolerance, good temper and sympathy – they are what matter really, and if the human race is not to collapse they must come to the front before long. But for the moment they are not enough, their action is no stronger than a flower, battered beneath a military jack-boot. They want stiffening, even if the process coarsens them. Faith, to my mind, is a stiffening process, a sort of mental starch, which ought to be applied as sparingly as possible. I dislike the stuff. I do not believe in it, for its own sake, at all. Herein I probably differ from most people, who believe in Belief, and are only sorry they cannot swallow even more than they do. My law-givers are Erasmus and Montaigne, not Moses and St Paul. My temple stands not upon Mount Moriah but in that Elysian Field where even the immoral are admitted. My motto is: 'Lord, I disbelieve – help thou my unbelief.'

E. M. Forster (1879–1970), from *Two Cheers for Democracy*

Postscript

The Rt Revd Richard Yeo, *Abbot of Downside*

O Come, thou Wisdom, from on high,
Who orderest all things mightily;
To us the path of knowledge show
And teach us in her ways to go.

Advent antiphon for 17 December

O Come, thou Dayspring, come and cheer
Our spirits by thine advent here;
Disperse the gloomy clouds of night,
And death's dark shadows put to flight.

Advent antiphon for 21 December

❡ The 'O antiphons' are sung at Vespers during the last week of Advent, from 17 to 23 December. The second verse was translated from the Latin by John M. Neale (1818–66). The first verse was translated by a committee for the Episcopal Church, USA.

Index of Subjects

〜〜〜〜〜〜〜

Index of Contributors

Index of Authors and Sources

Acknowledgements

~~~~~~~~~~~~

Every effort has been made to locate copyright holders, although in a small number of cases this has proved impossible. We are grateful for permission to reprint the following copyright material. We also thank individuals who sent their own work.

Extracts from the Authorized Version of the Bible (The King James Bible), the rights in which are vested in the Crown, are reproduced by permission of the Crown's Patentee, Cambridge University Press.

Extracts from the New Revised Standard Version of the Bible, copyright 1989. Division of Christian Education of the National Council of the Churches of Christ in the United States of America. Used by permission. All rights reserved.

Extracts from the New Revised Standard Version of the Bible, Catholic edition, copyright 1989, 1993 by the Division of Christian Education of the National Council of the Churches of Christ in the United States of America. Used by permission. All rights reserved.

Extracts from the Revised Standard Version of the Bible, copyright 1952 (2nd edn, 1971) by the Division of Christian Education of the National Council of the Churches of Christ in the United States of America. Used by permission. All rights reserved.

Extracts from the Alternative Service Book 1980, copyright © The Central Board of Finance of the Church of England are reproduced with permission.

Extracts from The Book of Common Prayer, the rights in which are vested in the Crown, are reproduced by permission of the Crown's Patentee, Cambridge University Press.

Extracts from The Prayer Book as proposed in 1928 by permission of The Central Board of Finance of the Church of England.

The following items are arranged in order of appearance in the book:

Nicholas Elliott: from *With My Little Eye*, by permission of Michael Russell Publishers.

Horace: Granada Publishing for Ode 3.29, from *The Odes of Horace*, trans. James Michie.

Jacob Bronowski: Rita Bronowski for extract from *The Ascent of Man*.

Marcus Aurelius: from Marcus Aurelius, *Meditations*, trans. Maxwell Staniforth (London: Penguin Classics, 1964). Reproduced by permission of Penguin Books Ltd.

Ezra Pound: Faber & Faber Ltd for extract from *The Pisan Cantos*.

T. S. Eliot: Faber & Faber Ltd for T. S. Eliot, extract from 'The Music of Poetry' from *On Poetry and Poets*.

Louis de Bernières: extract from *Captain Corelli's Mandolin* by Louis de Bernières, published by Vintage. Reprinted by permission of The Random House Group Ltd.

Antoine de Saint-Exupéry: from *The Little Prince* by Anoine de Saint-Exupéry. Reprinted by permission of Harcourt Education Ltd.

Hugh Kingsmill: from Michael Holroyd, *The Best of Hugh Kingsmill* (Gollancz, 1970). By permission of the Revd Brooke Kingsmill-Lunn.

Bertolt Brecht: 'Das Wiedersehen,' from *Kalendergeschichten*, by permission of Reinbeck Verlag, Hamburg.

Shusaku Endo: *Silence*, by permission of Peter Owen Publishers, London.

The Bhagavad Gita: extract from *The Bhagavad Gita*, trans. Franklin Edgerton (Cambridge, Mass.: Harvard University Press). Copyright © 1944 by the President and Fellows of Harvard College. Copyright © renewed 1972 by Eleanor Hill Edgerton.

Isaiah Berlin: from *Political Ideas in the Twentieth Century*, reproduced by permission of Curtis Brown Group Ltd, London, on behalf of The Isaiah Berlin Literary Trust. Copyright © Isiah Berlin 1950, 1969.

T. S. Eliot: Faber & Faber Ltd for T. S Eliot, 'Little Gidding' (*Four Quartets*), from T. S. Eliot, *Collected Poems* 1909–1962.

Phil Ochs: lyric from 'There but for Fortune' by Phil Ochs, used by permission of Megan Lee Potter.

Donald Maitland: extract from *Diverse Times, Sundry Places*, The Alpha Press, 1996 © Donald Maitland.

Rudyard Kipling: 'If', by permission of A. P. Watt Ltd, on behalf of The National Trust for Places of Historical Interest or Natural Beauty.

Vincent Van Gogh: Thames & Hudson for extract from J. Van Gogh-Bonger, and C. de Dood, *The Complete Letters of Vincent Van Gogh*, copyright © Thames & Hudson 1958.

Stephen Spender: Faber & Faber Ltd for 'I Think Continually of Those Who Were Truly Great', from Stephen Spender, *Collected Poems*.

Roger McGough: for extract from '10.15 Thursday Morning, Memphis, Tennessee', from *Watchwords* (London: Jonathan Cape 1969).

G. W. Young: for 'High Hills', from *Gather the Fragments*, Cairns.

Adrian Mitchell: for 'William Blake Says: Every Thing That Lives is Holy'.

Ernest Hemingway: for extract from *A Moveable Feast* by Ernest Hemingway, published by Jonathan Cape. Reprinted by permission of The Random House Group Ltd.

Albert Scweitzer: by permission of Madame Rhena Schweitzer-Miller.

Laurence Housman: from Laurence Housman, *Brother Sun: Little Plays of St Francis*, published by Jonathan Cape. Used by permission of The Random House Group Ltd.

Rabindranath Tagore: Visva-Bharati for 'Their Love Brings You to My Heart'.

Isle Crawford: Quadrill Publishing for quotation from *Sensual Home*.

W. H. Davies: Mrs H. M. Davies Will Trust for 'Leisure', by W. H. Davies.

Dietrich Bonhoeffer: SCM Press for 'Miscellaneous Thoughts', Dietrich Bonhoeffer, *Letters and Papers from Prison* (enlarged edn) (1971).

Ted Hughes: *Wild Steelhead and Salmon Magazine* for interview with Ted Hughes.

Ted Hughes: Faber & Faber Ltd for 'Pike', from Ted Hughes, *Lupercal.*

Brian Patten: for 'Two Men from the Same Town'.

Jamie Pegge: for 'The Creation'.

Charles Morgan: Roger Morgan and the Scott Faris Association, for extract from Charles Morgan, Introduction, *The River Line.*

W. H. Auden: Faber & Faber Ltd for extract from *For The Time Being.*

Sean O'Casey: Macnoughton Lord and The Sean O'Casey Estate for extract from Sean O'Casey, 'The Bald Primaqueera' from *Blasts and Benedictions.*

Bhagavad Gita: Godsfield Press for extract from *The Illustrated Bhagavad Gita*, trans. Ranchor Prime.

Leonard Cheshire: The Bouverie Foundation and the Leonard Cheshire Foundation for extract from *The Hidden World.*

Fergal Keane: the *Independent* for extract from Fergal Keane, 'Phone Call after Phone Call', 17 September 2001.

John Macmurray: the estate of John Macmurray for extract from *Freedom in the Modern World* (London: Faber & Faber Ltd, 1932).

Stuart K. Hine: The Stuart Hine Trust and Kingsway's Thankyou Music, PO Box 75, Eastbourne, East Sussex BN23 6NW, UK. Worldwide (excluding North and South America). All rights reserved. Used by permission.

Claude Lévi-Strauss: excerpt from Claude Lévi-Strauss, *Structural Anthropology*, by permission of Perseus Books, New York.

Rt Revd Robert Runcie: James Runcie for extract from a sermon by Rt Revd Robert Runcie for the 550th anniversary of Queen's College, Cambridge.

Czeslaw Milosz and Robert Hass: for 'And Yet the Books', trans. Robert Hass.

Minnie Louise Haskins: Sheil Land Associates Ltd for 'The Gate of the Year'.

Philip Larkin: Faber & Faber Ltd for 'An Arundel Tomb', from Philip Larkin, *Collected Poems*.

W. B. Yeats: A. P. Watts Ltd, on behalf of Michael Yeats, for W. B. Yeats, 'He Wishes for the Cloths of Heaven'.

Albert Einstein: The Albert Einstein Archives, the Hebrew University of Jerusalem, for 'Mein Glaubensbekenntnis', trans. Barbara Harshav.

George Santayana: Constable & Robinson Ltd for extract from *The Realms of Being*, Book 3.

Maurice Chevalier: Robson Books, for quotation from David Bret, *Maurice Chevalier*.

Gösta Ågren: Gösta Ågren and David McDuff for 'Death's Secret', trans. David McDuff.

Marcel Proust: extract from *Remembrance of Things Past* by Marcel Proust, published by Chatto & Windus. Used by permission of the estate of Marcel Proust, the estate of the translator Terence Kilmartin and The Random House Group Ltd.

Mary Rae Campbell: the *Literary Review* for 'A Valentine' published February 1990.

Fanny Burney: Kate Chisholm for extract from *Fanny Burney: Her Life* by Kate Chisholm, published by Chatto & Windus. Reprinted by permission of The Random House Group Ltd.

Will Rogers: CMG Worldwide.

Donald Nicholl: extract from Donald Nicholl, *Holiness*, copyright © 1982, reproduced by permission of Darton, Longmann & Todd.

R. S. Thomas: Andreas Gwyndion Thomas for 'Arrival', from R. S. Thomas, *Collected Poems* (London: JM Dent).

Sheldon Vanauken: extract from Sheldon Vanauken, *A Severe Mercy*, reproduced by permission of Hodder & Staughton Ltd.

Peter Medawar: for extract from 'Creativity – Especially in Science' (1985), in D. Pyke (ed.) *The Threat and the Glory – Reflections on Science and Scientists* (Oxford: OUP, 1990). Reprinted by permission of Oxford University Press. Thanks to Lady Medawar and Charles Medawar.

E. M. Forster: the Provost and Scolars of King's College, Cambridge, and the Society of Authors, on behalf of the E. M. Forster estate, for extract from 'What I believe' from *Two Cheers for Democracy*.

Advent antiphon for 17 December: from *The Hymnal* 1940 of the Episcopal Church, USA, copyright © Church Pension Fund. Used by permission.